PAINT IT
YOURSELF

PAINT IT YOURSELF

The Complete Indoor House-Painting Book

by Lois Libien
& Margaret Strong

WILLIAM MORROW AND COMPANY, INC.

NEW YORK   1978

Library of Congress Cataloging in Publication Data

Libien, Lois.
    Paint it yourself.

    Includes index.
    1. House painting—Amateurs' manuals. 2. Interior decoration—Amateurs' manuals. I. Strong, Margaret, joint author. II. Title.
TT323.L5   645'.2   78-6692
ISBN 0-688-03289-3
ISBN 0-688-08232-4 pbk.

Printed in the United States of America.

First Edition

1   2   3   4   5   6   7   8   9   10

Contents

5

Introduction

WHY PAINT IT YOURSELF? Because it's cheaper and because nobody cares as much as you do about the outcome.

Why paint it yourself? So you won't have to wait around for the painters to come. One woman we know spent an entire week sitting in her apartment, afraid to budge out the door for fear she'd miss the landlord's painters. They finally arrived on Friday, set up their ladders and drop cloths and then exited for a long lunch that lasted until Monday—leaving her apartment unlivable in the interim. To make matters worse, they refused to paint the closets and insisted on using the same paint everywhere. She says she's going to be the first to buy a copy of this book.

Why paint it yourself? So you have control over the job. So you can use the very best paints and brushes and rollers and paint pads—because the best makes a difference in the long run. So you won't have to remove the paint and start all over again, which would take twice the time and cost you twice the money.

Why paint it yourself? So you can have the sweet satisfaction of knowing the job was done right.

Why paint it yourself? Because it's a lot easier than you may think it is.

Okay, if it's so easy, then why do you need this book?

You need it so you'll know what paint and equipment to use to get the best results possible. You need this book so you'll know how to *prepare* your walls and ceilings and floors and chairs and tables and chests and bookshelves, etc., the way they should be prepared *before* you paint. Because preparation makes all the difference in the world between a good paint job that will last as long as you still like the color, and a slipshod, mediocre, disappointing job that will make you wonder why you ever bothered to do it yourself.

If you had twenty years to practice and an endless array of walls, ceilings, chairs, and tables to practice on, you'd certainly stumble on the right, easy way to paint on your own. But we're assuming that you have some concern for the things you want to paint, and that you'd rather not mess them up or spend all your spare time redoing them. This book is to help you PAINT IT YOURSELF—the right way, right off—with no stumbling, no confusion, no trial and error.

Way back some forty or fifty years ago, you could get away with using the same can of paint for everything in or out of the house—but no more. Nowadays, the paint manufacturers make a paint for nearly every purpose, and often not just one paint for every purpose, but two or three or four or more. If you have ever walked into one of those enormous paint supermarkets that dot the suburban byways of this nation, you know what we mean. You could go mad reading all those labels to find what you need. And, unfortunately, in some of those mammoth paint stores, you get little help from the clerks, whose only function seems to be to make change, not to serve the individual needs of each trusting customer. There are, of course, many exceptions. We've found some wonderful small, well-stocked paint stores where the proprietors seem to know just about everything there is to know about paint and its application and where there seems to be a sincere desire to impart knowledge. Our hats are off to these paint dealers! But if you can't find such help, you can rely on the chapters that follow.

What you won't learn in this book is how to paint exteriors —exterior walls, patios, porches, and the like. That, we decided, is another book. We do tell, however, how to paint both sides of your front door—interior and exterior—because we feel that is your introduction to the inside of your home.

We'd like to take this opportunity to thank all the wonderful people who helped us learn how to PAINT IT YOURSELF. Most sincerely, we want to thank the proprietors of some of those wonderful small, well-stocked paint stores we mentioned—and, for their patience and technical expertise, the people at Benjamin Moore & Company, Minwax Company, Boyle-Midway, Pergament Paint Company, Sherwin-Williams, and Haeuser's Shellac.

—LOIS LIBIEN AND MARGARET STRONG

I

Paint, Primers, etc. –What You Need to Know

HERE ARE TWO very important facts about paint:

- Paint is a mixture of pigment and binder, thinned with a solvent or water to form a liquid.

- Most paint dries through the evaporation or oxidation of its liquid (though there are a few paints that dry by a chemical process).

The truth is, you don't need to know these things to paint. Some people, *good* painters, never find out *how* paint dries. But they know that it does dry, that it takes an hour or two hours or longer to dry, and that you don't touch wet paint.

What I'm saying is, you don't have to know very much about paint in order to paint. On the other hand, you should know *something*.

Granted, the subject is confusing. No longer can you use the same can of paint for every job in or out of the house. It seems hard to believe that such a feat once was possible. But it was—and not too many years ago at that.

Today if you walk into any large paint store, you'll find aisle after aisle after aisle of paint for every imaginable purpose. Paint for walls, floors, ceilings, tile, metal, cement . . . even bathtubs. Textured paint. Spray paint. High-gloss, semigloss, and flat paint. Epoxy paint. Alkyds. Latexes. Primers. Sealers. Stains. Etc. Etc. Etc.

Occasionally, if you give the impression that you're puzzled, you'll be assisted by an experienced salesperson who will direct you to the perfect paint for the job you're planning. But don't count on it. The first time I walked into a paint store, the clerk—the only one in the store at the time—knew little more about paint than I did (that is, next to nothing), and I don't think my experience is unique.

Painting can be a big job, requiring a chunk of your time and a lot of preparation. And yet, no matter what you do or how well you do it, you won't get the results you want unless you have the right paint for the job.

So it helps to know something about paint before ever walking into that paint store.

TWO KINDS OF PAINT

There are so many different kinds of interior paint on the market that it boggles the mind. Our only defense is to simplify.

We'll start off by saying there are only two kinds of interior paint: latex paint and alkyd paint. (That's about as generalized a statement as saying there are only two kinds of people in the world.)

Latex paint is thinned with water and cleans up easily with soap (or detergent) and water. Alkyd (pronounced *al*-kid) paint is thinned with turpentine or some other, similar solvent, which also must be used for the clean-up. But there's a bit more to it than that.

1. *Alkyd paint* is oil-base paint. We don't mean to insult your

12

intelligence by mentioning this, but paint dealers tell us that people are always asking for "all-*kide*" paint and then being surprised to learn it's not another kind of latex paint. It's not. It's oil-base paint made with a synthetic resin or chemical blend that takes the place of linseed oil. Alkyds came into use in the late 1930s as a substitute for linseed oil in interior paints because linseed oil "yellowed" on the wall. Today, all interior oil-base paints are alkyd paints. There are still a few exterior oil-base paints made with linseed oil, however. Outdoors, the yellowing doesn't occur. The ultraviolet rays of the sun keep the linseed oil from turning color.

Since I literally fell asleep reading a book on alkyds, I won't go into minute detail. It's enough to say that alkyd paint is more stain-resistant, gives a higher gloss, and takes hard scrubbing better than latex paint. And it's least affected by temperature changes during painting. For example, if you're painting the interior of an unheated house in the winter, it's a good idea to use alkyd paint. Latex paint shouldn't be used indoors anyplace where the temperature may fall below 45° F. while you're painting.

However, alkyd paint is not entirely odor-free, although some alkyds smell better than others. (Margaret tells me she pried open one can of alkyd paint and then closed it again, quickly, because of the smell.) Alkyd paint also takes longer to dry than latex paint, even though it's an improvement on the old oil-base paints that took days and days to dry.

But the worst thing about using alkyd paint is the cleaning up. Flammable solvent must be used to clean away smudges and drips, and even splatters on your skin. Solvent must also be used for cleaning brushes, rollers, paint pads, etc. All cleaning cloths should be disposed of immediately. (The best way to dispose of solvent-soaked cloths is to put them in a water-filled container on top of your garbage can with a note attached, telling the garbage collector exactly what they are. Never throw them down an incinerator.) Flammable solvent is also used to thin alkyd paint.

Before I tell you more about alkyd paint than you ever wanted to know, here's some relief. Alkyds and all solvent-thinned paint

13

stand a good chance of becoming obsolete within the next five or ten years. Sources in the paint industry predict that latex paints will completely take over. The reason: Environmentalists are kicking up a storm over those flammable solvents, which pollute the atmosphere. As you can imagine, paint industry chemists are working overtime to formulate latex paints that are stronger, glossier, and more scrubbable than alkyd paints are now.

2. *Latex paints* are just about odor-free. They go on easily, dry quickly (some dry in thirty minutes), and cover effectively. Also, they're long-lasting, they retain their color and gloss, and they touch up easily. If you've missed a few spots, you needn't worry. The fresh paint will blend in beautifully.

But the best thing about latex paint is the cleanup. As long as you quickly clean away drips and splatters and clean your equipment before the paint hardens, it's a dream. Just use soap and water. As one nonprofessional painter to another, I recommend using latex paint wherever possible. It's good for just about everything except porcelain, ceramic tile, and laminated plastic, which require special paint.

However, sometimes it really is better to use alkyd paints. As of this writing, there's still no really excellent interior latex enamel or high-gloss paint, and semigloss alkyd paint is probably more scrubbable than its latex equivalent. Glossy alkyds still work better in rooms where water is used and splashed about (kitchens, bathrooms, laundry rooms) and on trim, such as windowsills and doors, that is apt to be scrubbed frequently.

(Incidental information: There are a few paints known as latex alkyd. They're usually low-quality latex paints fortified with alkyds to give them more capacity to cover. Even though they clean up easily with water, they're not very popular.)

If you don't know what kind of paint you have on a surface, don't worry. You can use alkyd paint over latex paint or latex over alkyd without trouble. But, if the paint seems *at all glossy*, it's absolutely necessary to sand or "degloss" the surface before applying any kind of paint whatsoever. The prior glossy or semigloss paint is too smooth—it doesn't have enough "tooth"—for the new paint to adhere properly. We tell how to degloss in Chapter IV and elsewhere throughout the book as well.

FINISHES

We've just mentioned high-gloss and semigloss paints. Both latex and alkyd paints are made in three main types of finishes— flat, semigloss, and high-gloss. Their names are more or less self-explanatory. Here are some of their characteristics:

1. *Flat* paints give a dull, flat, glare-resistant finish most often used on walls and ceilings in bedrooms and living rooms—and on trim that gets moderate wear. Flat paints are washable, but not as washable as the glossier paints. If there's a bumpy, uneven surface you want to paint, use flat paint. It acts as camouflage, making the unevenness less obvious.

Most of the flat paint sold is latex paint.

2. *Semigloss* paints give a little more shine than flat paints and are more washable and stain-resistant. They're used mainly in kitchens and bathrooms and for trim. Alkyd semigloss paint is probably more scrubbable than latex.

3. *High-gloss* paints give a hard, shiny finish that takes a lot of wear and frequent scrubbings. They're particularly recommended for cabinets, chairs and other furniture, toys, and trim. Some manufacturers make a high-gloss interior latex paint, but as of this writing, high-gloss alkyds still work better.

There are other finishes, too. In between flat and semigloss are two finishes that are sometimes called velvet and eggshell. Satin is another finish description that is used differently by various manufacturers. A good paint dealer will show you samples of the finishes he has in stock and provide information on their use.

PRIMERS

A primer is the first coat that's applied to a surface. It's sometimes called a base coat, or an undercoater, or a sealer or conditioner. What it does is coat a porous surface so the paint won't soak in, and coat a slick surface so the paint will take hold better. Some people take shortcuts and use a first coat of their top-coat paint instead of using a primer, figuring they'll save themselves some work and money. Sometimes they can get away with it, sometimes not. But they may be wasting money; primers are generally less expensive than top-coat paint.

There are five instances in which using a primer is essential:

- When painting new wallboard, bare wood, or any previously unpainted surface;

- When painting over a slick surface such as plastic or glass;

- When painting light over dark;

- When painting over badly stained or heavily patched surfaces, or over brightly patterned wallpaper that is likely to show through top-coat paint;

- And when you want a really, really good paint job that will last for years and years.

You'll find all you need to know about that last point in Chapter V (How to Paint Ceilings and Walls). It's enough for now to say that when you really want a top-notch, long-lasting job, it's best to prepare the surface properly and make sure it's cleaned, sanded, and primed before the top one or two coats of paint go on.

A few more words about primers: They are almost always white, but you can tint them toward the color of your top coat (halfway toward the top-coat color is about the most you can expect to tint it) by mixing in some of the top-coat paint or some universal color, which comes in a tube or a can at your paint dealer's. Universal color is a pigment formulation, available in an array of basic colors, that can be used to tint almost any paint, alkyd or latex. When using it, follow the directions on the label. Oh, yes—universal color shouldn't be used as paint . . . it's tint. If you hesitate about doing this job yourself, ask your paint dealer to do it for you.

Basically, there are three types of primers: latex primers, alkyd primers, and pigmented shellac-base primers. Of course, there are specialized primers and sealers for just about everything, and we describe them throughout the book. But basically, that's it.

Alkyd and latex primers apply in the same way as alkyd and latex paint. That is, you can use a roller, a paint pad, a spray gun, or a brush and follow the directions for painting as described in Chapters III and IV. It's not necessary to use latex primer with latex paint and alkyd primer with alkyd paint—but you'll probably get better results if you do. For the *best* results, choose your top-coat paint first, read the label thoroughly, and then buy the primer that's recommended for use with it . . . the one that's made by the same manufacturer. That top-coat paint and that primer were literally made for each other.

Shellac-base primers are used mainly as stain-killers. In fact, if you go into a paint store and ask for stain-killer, chances are you'll be handed a can of shellac-base primer. Two of the best-known brands are B-I-N and Enamelac. Technically, they are primer-sealers. They seal sappy wood that bleeds through other paints and finishes, and they are also good for covering wood or metal that is discolored by tar or creosote, as well as wood charred by fire; they also seal and prime stained plaster and patterned wallpaper. On nonporous hard surfaces, such as plastic, glass, shiny metal, ceramic tile, etc., to which paint doesn't easily adhere, the pigmented shellac primer will bond securely so the surface can be finished with whatever paint you choose. Denatured alcohol, rather than turpentine or mineral spirits, is used to thin these primers and also for cleaning up when the job is done.

SPECIALIZED PAINTS

Calcimine.   Calcimine is a water-thinned paint that was used mainly for ceilings some years back. If you live in an older place and suspect that the ceilings have calcimine on them, you must remove the calcimine before painting. Not even a new coat of calcimine will go on over an old one. It is easily removed, however. Just scrub it off with detergent and hot water. (To test if it really *is* calcimine on the ceiling, try washing an inconspicuous corner. If it washes off, it's calcimine.)

Ceiling paint.   You can use wall paint on your ceilings. Many people do. But if your ceilings are yellowed with age or cigar smoke, or if they've been patched and repatched, you'll get better coverage with ceiling paint. It has more pigment—and therefore more hiding power, as well as more glare-resistance—than other paints. It's also supposed to drip less. Yes, you can use ceiling paint on walls, but it's too dull for most tastes. Also, it isn't as washable as wall paints. (No one is supposed to get fingerprints on the ceiling!) Most ceiling paints have just a touch of blue in them for added glare-resistance. They come in both latexes and alkyds.

Deck and floor enamels.   These are tough, durable enamels meant to take heavy traffic, scuffing, and repeated scrubbings. They can be used on wood, concrete, and metal surfaces as well as on floors—but always be sure to read the directions on the label before painting. Very often, special preparation—and sometimes a primer—is necessary. Deck and floor enamels come in latex, alkyd, and polyurethane paints. (See Enamel, page 19.)

Dripless paints.   A few years ago, dripless latex paints were considered the hottest thing on the market. No longer. These paints are made in a thick, yogurt-like consistency designed for one-coat coverage. But they just aren't dripless. If they're thinned,

18

they don't cover in one coat. Undiluted, they tend to "glop" if the application is the slightest bit careless.

Enamel. Technically, enamel isn't paint. Exactly what it is is a point everyone seems to skirt around, so let's just say that enamel is a smooth, hard, washable pigmented finish that will take a lot of wear and tear.

There are flat, semigloss, and high-gloss enamels in both alkyd and latex formulations. However, they are always labeled ENAMEL—and, for example, a high-gloss alkyd *paint* is something different from a high-gloss alkyd enamel. (Did I lose you?) Enamel is also usually specifically formulated and labeled for a specific job—whether it be painting wood furniture, metal, masonry floors, or whatever. The primer that should be used with it is *enamel undercoater,* which can also be used under paint. Ordinary alkyd or latex primers, however, do not work well under enamel.

Enamels are applied with brush, mohair roller, or pad or spray apparatus. But when using high-gloss enamel, brush or spray it on. When brushing it on, you should load your brush more fully than you would if you were using paint. Then flow the enamel on the surface and brush it out less than you would brush paint. Enamel dries quickly, so any runs or sags should be remedied immediately.

Epoxy paint. This is probably the toughest, hardest coating you can find and, like enamel, it's not paint. It's a "catalytic coating." Unlike latex and alkyds, it dries and hardens (to a glasslike finish) by means of a chemical process instead of by the evaporation or oxidation of liquid. It's so difficult to apply, and so volatile and flammable, however, that it's necessary to be extremely careful when using it. (There are more do's and don'ts on the epoxy label than on almost any other.) Always work in a well-ventilated room and follow directions exactly. In fact, read the label several times through before even opening the can.

Epoxies are used to paint porcelain (old toilets, bathtubs,

etc.) and appliances as well as masonry and metals. True epoxy paint comes in two containers; the contents must be mixed together before use. Some are meant to be used immediately after mixing, while others require waiting for an hour or two before use. (Epoxy-*type* enamels come in one container, but are not considered as strong as true epoxies.)

Epoxies won't go on over other paints, but they will cover old epoxy. They can be brushed, sprayed, or rolled on, but don't plan to use the equipment again. It will be impossible to clean. Once epoxy begins hardening, it doesn't stop until the hardening action is completed. So don't even stop to answer the phone before you've cleaned away all drips and smudges.

Lacquers. These are very fast-drying, highly flammable paints meant for small surfaces, usually furniture, that call for an extremely hard finish. Because they dry so quickly, lacquers get sticky on the brush and are best applied as an aerosol spray. If you do brush on lacquers, apply them in two thin coats rather than one thicker coat. Follow the directions on the label exactly and be sure to work in a well-ventilated room. (As an amateur, I prefer enamels and other finishes and leave the lacquers to the professionals!)

Spray paints. Those small cans of spray paint you'll find in almost any paint store seem handy—and they are, if you have a small job to do. But I'd think twice about using them. First of all, they're expensive. Each can actually contains very little paint. If you're painting something sizable, you'd do better to buy, borrow, or rent a spray gun. But be aware that spray-painting indoors is a messy job and no matter how careful you are, you run the risk of overspray (in the form of small specks of paint where you don't want them). If at all possible, it's best to take the work out-of-doors or down to the basement—or build yourself a spraying booth, as described in Chapter III.

Textured paints. Available in both latexes and alkyds, textured paints are flat and heavy-bodied and give a beautifully textured effect over practically any surface. They're particularly good for camouflaging an imperfect surface and will effectively cover patching. When applying textured paints with a brush, you can create a swirl effect by twisting the handle of the brush back and forth. If you use a roller, you get a heavy stipple. You can comb the paint (with a comb), whisk it with a whisk broom, or dab it with a sponge or crumpled newspaper to pattern the surface while the paint is still wet. Sand-finish paint, which contains granules of perlite or some other gritty substance, dries to a sandy finish resembling concrete. (See Chapter V for more information on textured paints.)

There are also stains and sealers and shellacs and varnishes for finishing and refinishing floors as well as furniture (Chapters IX and X). There are paints especially formulated for use on metal (Chapter VIII) and use on brick, cement, and other masonry (Chapter VII). There are mildew-resistant paints, fluorescent paints, fire-retardant paints.

And on ad infinitum, whatever you need, whatever you want. And if you're not absolutely sure exactly what paint you do need for the surface you want to paint, buy your paint from a dealer who really knows enough to help you. Don't just walk into a paint store and pick a can off the shelf.

HOW MUCH PAINT WILL YOU NEED?

If you can do simple arithmetic, you can easily estimate the amount of paint you'll need for almost any job.

Walls. With a yardstick or a tape measure, measure the distance around the room—its perimeter. Then measure the height of the walls, floor to ceiling. To get the square footage of the room, multiple the perimeter by the height. Then divide the result by 400 square feet, which is the area usually covered by one gallon of paint. (Most labels tell you the square footage the particular type of paint will cover.)

Trim. If you're using a different type of paint for the trim, subtract the total square footage of the trim (doors, windows, etc.) from the square footage of the room before you divide the result by the amount of paint each gallon will cover.

Generally you can figure 21 square feet for each door and 15 square feet for each average window.

Estimating the square footage of built-in cabinets and book-shelves can be trickier. For example, you'll probably be painting the undersides of the shelves as well as the top surfaces. Just multiply length by height to determine square footage, and then buy a little more paint than you've estimated.

Floors and ceilings. To find the square footage of floors and ceilings, multiply the width of the room by its length. Divide the answer by the number of square feet each gallon of paint will cover to determine how much paint you'll need.

Here's what your arithmetic will look like if you're painting a bedroom 12 feet by 16 feet with an eight-foot-high ceiling. There are two doors in the room, and two windows. The walls will be painted with flat latex paint; the trim with glossy alkyd paint; and the ceiling with ceiling paint.

The perimeter of the room is:

$$12 + 12 + 16 + 16 \text{ ft., or } 56 \text{ ft.}$$

The wall area, including doors and windows, is:

$$56 \text{ ft.} \times 8 \text{ ft. (height)} = 448 \text{ sq. ft.}$$

With two doors (each 21 sq. ft.) and two windows (each 15 sq. ft.), the total trim area is:

$$42 \text{ sq. ft.} + 30 \text{ sq. ft.} = 72 \text{ sq. ft.}$$

The wall area excluding trim is:

$$448 \text{ sq. ft.} - 72 \text{ sq. ft.} = 376 \text{ sq. ft.}$$

The ceiling area of the 12 ft. × 16 ft. room is:

$$12 \text{ ft.} \times 16 \text{ ft.} = 192 \text{ sq ft.}$$

The amount of paint you need for *one coat* is:

For walls: $376 \div 400 = .94$ gallon   Buy a gallon.
For trim: $72 \div 400 = .18$ gallon   Buy a quart.
For the ceiling: $192 \div 400 = .48$ gallon   Buy two quarts.

HOW MUCH PAINT TO BUY

It never hurts to buy a little more paint than you need and to buy it all at once, from the same dealer. I'm not trying to sell more paint; I'm trying to cut down on heartache.

Paint is made in batches, and if you run out to buy a little more paint of the same color, it may—or may not—be from the same batch. Even if you have the batch number of the paint you're using, you're never sure the paint will still be in stock. The paint now on the shelf may have been made 23 batches later —with ever-so-slight a variation in color from batch to batch.

What if you're good at math and are able to estimate *exactly* how much paint you need? Well, you won't always be accurate. If your walls are more porous than you thought, you'll probably need more paint than you figured for the first coat. (Porous walls soak up paint.) The same is true if you're painting light over dark, or making a color change. (You're more likely to put on a thicker coat of paint.) These problems can be avoided if you use a primer, however. The primer will seal the porous wall and cover the dark paint so that you *can* accurately gauge the amount of paint you'll use.

Whatever you do, be sure you have enough paint in the can at least to cover an entire wall. Don't stop in the middle of the wall and begin again with a new can of paint. Chances are nine out of ten that the colors won't match, not even if you're using white paint!

BARGAIN PAINT AND CHEAP PAINT

Is the best paint really necessary?
The answer is yes.

Buy the very best paint you can afford. Paint is really the least expensive part of the paint job, considering all the time and preparation that go into the finished product. As you'll discover in Chapters I and II, preparation for the paint application is 90 percent of the work and the actual application of paint only 10 percent. So even if a gallon of top-quality paint costs fifteen dollars, it's relatively inexpensive when you consider the cost of your time and labor. (Just think what you'd pay a union painter to do the job!)

Is the most expensive paint really the best paint?

Usually, yes.

With paint, price probably is the best way of differentiating high-quality paint from low. Say, for example, that one can of paint is selling for seven dollars more than another can of the same type of paint. That is a big difference and the higher-priced can probably contains more of whatever it takes to make that paint durable and washable. It stands to reason that something must be lacking in the cheaper paint. The manufacturer has to be saving himself something somewhere to make a profit at the lower price.

But even the best, most expensive paints sometimes go on sale. Great. And professional painters tell me that if the difference in price between two cans of paint is only a dollar or two, buy the cheaper one. Both paints are probably of the same quality, and the price difference may be due to the different costs of advertising and distribution.

ALWAYS BE SURE TO READ
THE LABELS

Again, no insult meant to your intelligence. It's just that so many of us are tempted to pry open the can of paint and begin the job that we don't study the fine print on the label. And that's a big mistake.

The label should tell you all you need to know about the

paint: how to prepare your surfaces, whether or not you'll need a primer, what equipment should be used, how many square feet the paint in the can will cover. The label will also tell you how long it will be before the paint is dry, how to clean up when you're through, and if there are any hazards involved in the use of the paint. It's wise to heed *all* warnings and never ignore the instructions.

How to pour paint so you won't obscure the directions: When you pour paint out of the original can into a bucket or a roller tray, always pour from the side away from where the directions are printed on the label. You may want to read those directions again later while you're working.

STIR THE PAINT BEFORE YOU BEGIN

Stirring is the last step before you paint, and it's an important step because all paint absolutely does need stirring.

By stirring, we *don't* mean shaking the can. Latex paints, polyurethanes, shellacs, and varnishes should never be shaken, or you'll create air bubbles that can last as long as four or five days.

When you buy the paint, ask the dealer to stir it up for you on a machine he usually keeps behind the counter. Then, even if you begin painting immediately upon returning home, stir it up again. Paint is that sort of substance; it settles.

Here's the most effective way to stir; it's a method the professionals call "boxing." (In addition to your can of paint, you'll need another can the same size or larger, or a paint bucket. It's also a good idea to spread newspapers or drop cloths over the floor before you begin.)

Here's how to "box" paint:
1. Pour off about ⅔ of the paint from the original can into the second can or bucket.

25

2. Then stir the remaining paint in the original can, using the paint stick most dealers give you free of charge when you buy paint. Go all the way down to the bottom of the can to stir up the settled pigment, and stir thoroughly until there are no signs of color separation.

3. Now pour back the ⅔ can of paint you've poured off, and stir again.

4. Last, pour the paint (directions side up) back and forth from one can or bucket to the other to mix it completely. Do this several times.

When you're finished, you can begin painting. But don't throw the paint stick away. You'll need it to stir up the paint again from time to time as you use it.

ALWAYS WORK IN A WELL-VENTILATED ROOM

Paint is toxic. While some paints are more toxic than others, *all wet paint is toxic*. So, even if you're using the most harmless latex paint available, be sure you're working in a well-ventilated room. Inhaling the fumes from paints and solvents can cause dizziness, fatigue, headaches, nausea, and even severe illness. So be sure to keep a window open while you work.

Keep the paint out of the reach of children. If they're young and curious, they probably can't wait to dip their hands into your paint trays and take a taste of that creamy substance. It's probably best to send small children to Grandma's for the weekend while you paint, or wait until they're asleep for the night.

Also keep pets away from paint and don't let them into a freshly painted room until the paint is good and dry. Pet birds, especially, are affected by paint fumes.

Important: Don't smoke while you're painting or using a solvent. Avoid smoking or using paint or solvent near a flame even if the paint is supposed to be nonflammable.

26

STORING PAINT

When you've finished the paint job, what do you do with the paint that's left over?

If there's just a little left, it's probably not worth saving. But if you think you might want to repaint or touch up with the same color and type of paint sometime in the future—and if you have sufficient storage space—you might want to save the can with the label intact and with a notation on the can telling what you used the paint for, and when.

If more than half a can of paint is left, you can safely store it. But make sure the lid is tightly sealed; clean the rim with a damp rag and then tap the lid firmly but gently with a hammer so it's on good and tight.

Paint is best stored in a cool, dry place. It may deteriorate if it freezes, though not necessarily. Never store paint or solvents where there is any danger of combustion.

How long can you store paint? For months, and sometimes for even a year or two. But when you reopen the can, don't be surprised to see that a film known as "skin" has formed on top. Skim this off as carefully as you can; never stir it into the paint.

There is a way to prevent the formation of skin. Before re-sealing and storing the can, pour a very thin layer of water or linseed oil onto the surface of the paint. Use water for latex paints and linseed oil for alkyds. Then seal the can very tightly and be careful not to jiggle it as you place it on the shelf. Next time you use the paint, skim off as much of the protective layer as possible instead of stirring it in.

ASK YOUR PAINT DEALER

As you plan your paint job, you'll discover you have more questions than you can find answers for in any printed material, even in this book.

Ask those questions! And don't begin painting until you've

found the answers. In fact, don't even buy your paint until you have the answers—specific answers for your specific paint job.

Whom do you ask? Ask a good paint dealer. If he's really good, he can tell you all you need to know, and maybe more. You probably will have to shop around a bit to find him, but he does exist. The people who manufacture the paint a dealer sells go to a lot of trouble to see that he knows just about everything there is to know about their paint. They *want* him to be able to answer your questions. They *want* you to be able to do a beautiful job. There's no altruism to it. They want you to be satisfied with their brand so that you'll keep on buying it and they can stay in business.

And if you can't find him, bone up on the subject of paint thoroughly yourself; use our index for reference and become an addict of label reading.

II

Color:
How to Choose It
& Use It

The kind of paint you choose for ceilings, walls, trim, furniture, or whatever—whether to use latex or alkyd, flat or high-gloss—really *must* depend on certain physical considerations, such as what the surface is made of, its location, whether it will be exposed to water, high heat, heavy wear and tear, etc.

But *the* only criterion for selecting a particular color of paint is whether or not YOU want to live with it.

The "you" in the last sentence is emphasized for a reason. Take a look at almost any book or magazine article about painting and you'll find certain "rules" for choosing and using color. These essays on the subject of color are almost always illustrated by a color wheel and include complicated instructions for achieving harmonious color schemes. A number of concepts are introduced. Concepts such as "complementary harmony" (based on colors that are directly opposite each other on the color wheel) and "split mutual complementary harmony" (based on a series of five colors that adjoin each other on the wheel, plus the complementary of the third color in the series). And more, much more. In fact, there are so many different possibilities deemed "harmonious" that in the end the only reasonable conclusion to be drawn is that any combination of colors at all "works"—

assuming you study the way they look together and like it.

Then there is the inevitable list of "do's and don'ts," usually warning the reader both against the use of too *much* color ("confusing," the writer says) and too little ("boring"). But haven't you found that some of the cheeriest, most inviting rooms you've ever seen were a veritable hodgepodge of riotous color? And that sometimes the single-color room—everything done in creamy ivory, for example, or shades of pale, grayed green—wasn't boring at all, but a haven of well-ordered calm?

You and I and my neighbor down the street all have favorite colors—the ones we want to see around us day in and day out. But it's doubtful that we'd all want the same thing. Someone I know has done a room all in red. She loves it. As for me, it's a nice place to visit, but I wouldn't want to live there. She probably feels the same about my basic beige living room. Color is such a personal thing.

That's exactly why we feel that rules about color are the kind that are made to be broken. So, better than a list of do's and don'ts for choosing and using color, we believe, is a discussion of how different colors "telegraph" different messages—how those colors affect a room and the objects in it. The information isn't intended to change anyone's color preferences, only to help in gauging final effects.

MESSAGES SENT BY VARIOUS COLORS

Warm colors. Yellows, golds, oranges, reds—these are the colors we associate with heat. Sunlight, for example, at least *seems* to have a golden glow. Flames are red, orange, yellow. And so on.

Warm colors, especially *bright* warm colors (as opposed to pastel or muted versions) are lively and gay. They seem to come forward and thus make a room appear somewhat smaller than it actually is. They're *too* forward for some people; and, indeed, it is possible to feel intruded upon by large areas of strong, warm color.

Warm colors, whether bright or muted, pastel or dark, tend to cheer and warm a room. In fact, the relative warmth or coolness of a color is one of the most important factors to consider when painting walls and ceilings. A living room, for example, with a sunny, southern exposure might, if you paint it orange, feel uncomfortably *hot,* especially in summer. The effect is purely psychological, of course, but it's still a potent one. (That same orange, incidentally, might be just the thing to warm up a room that gets little sun.)

Cool colors. Blue is the coolest color. Green can be cool if it has a lot of blue or gray in it (yellow-green is warmer). Purple, which is a mixture of blue and red, is cooler if the blue predominates, warmer if it tends toward red. Blue-gray and gray are cool (think of the winter sea and sky). So are the grayed beiges.

Whereas warm colors come forward, cool colors recede and tend to make a room seem larger. While warm colors heat up a room and its ambience, cool colors calm and quiet it. Just as some people can't tolerate the "raucousness" of strong warm color, others are unnerved by the icy reserve of an environment done all in cool colors. And of course, just as intense warm color in a sunny room may "feel" too hot for comfort, cool color in a room facing north may result in psychological shivers.

Bright colors—whether bright and warm or bright and cool —are powerful. Some people find them to be overpowering, though dynamic, aggressive types may feel right at home surrounded by vivid hues.

Use very bright color on the walls and the ceiling and the effect can be charmingly naïve (think of a red, yellow, and white children's room)—or, if not handled skillfully, results could be "garish." On the other hand, if all the other decorative elements work well together, intense color can be enormously sophisticated. (If you doubt it, take a look through any issue of *House & Garden.* Or think of the electric blues, vivid yellows and riveting pinks of a Matisse painting.)

31

Many color experts warn the novice decorator away from intense color on walls and ceiling. For one thing, they say, most people are likely to tire of a bright color more quickly than they would a softer, muted shade. For another, very bright color is considered too "active" (read "stimulating") for rooms where quiet activities—such as sleeping, eating, studying, or conversing —are engaged in. (That doesn't leave much; perhaps the ball-room, for those who have one, or a rumpus room.) Finally, since bright color begs for attention, it may make more noticeable any surface irregularities on walls. Which is not to say you shouldn't use bright color if you like it; only that you should think a bit about what you're getting into.

Muted colors—"dusty" roses, blues, and greens, old golds, maroons, etc.—are softer, toned-down versions of the brights. Muted colors can be warm and soft or cool and soft. The important thing about them is that they lack the hard "pure" edge of the brights. And indeed, their muted quality is the result of some other color having been added to the paint formula. (Bright red, for example, can be muted with the addition of some green or brown or black.)

Some people find muted colors, especially the darker ones, to be dull, drab, even depressing. Then again, other people love the restraint and sophistication of these shades. In a sense, an appreciation for these colors is acquired (like a taste for olives). It is known that very young children respond most strongly and positively to bright, pure colors (especially red); a liking for muted color seems to come only with maturity.

Color experts often suggest that muted shades, whether light or dark, warm or cool, are more in keeping with traditional decor than the crashing brights which can be so effective with contemporary or "modern" furnishings. Keep it in mind, but remember that like just about every other rule concerning color, this one can be broken, sometimes with marvelous results.

Light colors—most of them, anyway—contribute a fresh, airy feeling. Light colors seem to "expand." A small room painted a light color seems to be more spacious than a room of identical dimensions painted a darker, stronger version of that same color.

Dark colors, of course, work in the opposite way. Used on walls and ceilings, a dark color will make a room seem to "close up." Does this mean you should never paint a small room a dark color? Not at all. The opposite of fresh and airy isn't necessarily "oppressive." It could be delightfully "cozy" instead.

Whites.   There are literally hundreds of different colors light enough to be called white or off-white. They range from true whites of various intensities to whites with the slightest blush of pink or peach, to palest ivory, bone, and eggshell, to whites that veer off in the direction of blue, green, gray. (I once moved into an apartment painted an odd grayed white which my daughter promptly christened "clam-color.")

White is a neutral. It "goes with" anything. Most people know this and a few play it safe by opting for white time and time again.

It *is* hard to make a mistake with white. It doesn't clash with rugs and furnishings no matter what color they may be (but don't forget that of all the different whites, some will look better with certain colors than others). White is a good choice for brightening rooms with few or no windows (though a soft yellow would do almost as well). There's nothing like white to set off the fresh green of plants. And if you happen to have inherited several pieces of hulking dark wood furniture, white walls will lessen the total "weightiness" of the room.

Certain all-white rooms can be startlingly dramatic, or romantic, depending on the furnishings. But otherwise, white adds very little in the way of interest. It provides a neutral backdrop and not much else.

HOW TO PLAY TRICKS WITH COLOR

Now you already know that warm color on walls makes the room itself seem more cheerful and warmer (a good thing to keep in mind in these days of soaring fuel bills) and that cool color does the opposite. You also know that light colors, especially light cool colors, seem to enlarge a room, while dark colors —dark warm colors in particular—tend to make a room feel smaller. There are several other ways in which color can be used to alter our perceptions of a room.

Low ceilings, the only kind "they" seems to make anymore, will seem higher the lighter they are. This may account at least in part for the popularity of the paints that go by the name of "ceiling whites." A flat dead white (though some have a touch of blue in their makeup), these paints make a ceiling so unobtrusive that it practically vanishes.

High ceilings. Many people don't consider a high ceiling a problem unless it's *so* high it disturbs the proportions of a room. In such a case, the ceiling can be "lowered" in one of two ways: 1) You could choose a medium-to-dark color and use it on walls *and* ceiling, or 2) you could paint the ceiling a color that is somewhat darker than the walls. The first alternative will feel more comfortable and "natural" to most people because in nature, light comes from above—or at least "below" is not normally lighter than "above."

Conventionally, ceiling and walls are not painted the same color, though a serene, collected effect can be achieved that way. When you use two different colors, the ceiling color should stop, and the wall color begin, where ceiling and wall meet—except in those old-fashioned rooms where there is picture molding on the walls a foot or so below the ceiling. When that is the case, it is always best to bring the ceiling color down to the picture molding. Paint the picture molding itself the color of the walls.

Remember, there is no unbreakable rule that says all four walls of a room have to be the same color. In fact, in using two wall colors you may be able to give a room a feeling of better balance and pleasing proportions. For example:

The long, narrow room will seem wider and less like a "hallway" if the walls at each end (the short walls) are painted a color that is darker and warmer than the two long walls. In the same way, a long hallway will seem shorter if the wall at one or both ends is a darkish, warm color to contrast with the long, lighter walls and ceiling.

A perfectly square room with little in the way of eye-catching architectural detail can be a bore. This kind of room may be given interest by painting one wall a color that contrasts with the three others. And the shape of the room will seem to change considerably if each pair of opposing walls is painted to contrast with the other pair.

An unbalanced room where all the interest—doors, windows, and other architectural detail—is down at one end can be rebalanced in a couple of ways. One would be to paint the opposite uninteresting "blank" wall the same color as the one used on window frames, doorframes, and other trim surfaces at the far end of the room. The other, somewhat trickier course would be to paint the blank wall a brighter, warmer color than all the others.

Two wall colors can be used not only to right wrongs but also for drama, fun, and/or just because you want *more* color. For example, suppose you have a yen for a particular strong color but aren't sure you like it well enough to steep a whole room in it. One way to have your color without being overpowered by it is to use that strong color on one wall only. Just remember that the wall that gets the strong color treatment will become a focal point, the most important wall in the room. Be guided accordingly.

HOW TO COORDINATE PAINT
WITH WALLPAPER

Other variations on the theme of getting more color into a room can be worked out with wallpaper. For example, you could paint three walls and paper the fourth. In such a case, that fourth wall would predominate, so it probably shouldn't be the wall with the greatest number of doors and/or windows and other surface breaks. Or, you could paper three walls and paint the fourth. (Of course, you could paper four walls and the ceiling, too, for that matter, but this is a book about painting, so we'll limit this brief discussion to using paint and paper together.)

If you do opt for a combination of paint and paper, you should plan to do the painting first, the papering later. But before you do either, you must give thought to coordinating color.

To begin with, paint color should be determined by the colors in the paper, and not the other way around—so, make your paper selection first. Then you can decide what color to paint trim, ceiling, and any walls that will not be papered.

A standard way of coordinating paint and paper is to do trim and all other unpapered areas in the background color of the paper, or a very slightly darker or lighter version. You can't go too far wrong this way, provided that the background color is one you like well enough to use so importantly.

Of course, there are other possibilities. You can pick up any one of the colors in the paper and use it on trim and other surfaces to be painted. Just keep in mind that the color you choose will strongly affect the balance of the finished room.

For example, let's suppose that the paper is a floral stripe. The background color is peachy-beige, the print is navy blue, medium blue, yellow, and off-white. The background color, peachy-beige, doesn't appeal to you enough to use on trim and other unpapered areas. You could use the navy blue on those areas instead; if you do, the final effect will be closed-in and private, which could be what you want. Medium blue would lend a quiet, cool, but more open effect. Yellow would give gaiety and a much warmer atmosphere. And off-white would be fresh and, of course, safe.

Any of those colors would "work" in the sense of not clashing. But each would give an entirely different feel to the room. It's no easy task to visualize the final results of these combinations, but it's important to think them through carefully before deciding.

What if you've chosen one color for the trim and the unpapered wall areas, and a different color for the ceiling? What color should you paint the picture molding (assuming there is one)? The trim color? Or the color of the ceiling? Easiest would be to paint that picture molding in the color of the ceiling. Then you'd paint the ceiling, extending the color down to and including the picture molding, all in one operaion. (By contrast, if you try to match the molding to trim surfaces, you'll have to paint the ceiling first, then go back and do a very careful job of applying trim paint to the narrow molding. Unless you have your heart set on a certain effect, the extra effort probably won't be worth it.)

COLOR AS A UNIFYING ELEMENT

Don't overlook the unifying potential of color. Skillfully used, it can provide an easy continuity and flow from room to room. As a result, the entire house seems more a related whole than a collection of distinctly separate and unrelated "cells." (Have you ever been rather unpleasantly jolted by an abrupt change of color scheme from one room to the next in the home of someone you know?)

No, you don't have to use the same color on walls and ceilings in every single room in order to create a feeling of relatedness throughout the house. A one-color house could be an awful bore. But you could paint adjacent rooms in related colors: A terra-cotta room, for example, might open into a room with three walls the color of pale wheat and the fourth done in pumpkin, which might in turn open onto a hallway papered in rust, ivory, and deep-blue stripes. And so on.

You can also use color to lessen the contrast between various types of surfaces. Of course, contrast is often desirable, but a small room with, say, one brick wall, a fireplace on another wall, and wainscoting, built-in cabinets, and a series of doors and windows on the remaining walls might be very busy. You can subdue some of that busy-ness and make the room more of a piece by painting most of the different surfaces the same color.

37

HOW TO GET THE COLOR
YOU REALLY WANT

There is practically no limit to the number of different colors available to you. If the color you're looking for isn't already there in a container on your paint dealer's shelves, you can have it mixed up for you. Many, although not all paint stores do custom mixing. And there are color-mixing "systems" sold under brand names. You choose the color from a huge sample book, and the store mixes it for you by formula. These systems provide a very wide range of light to dark versions of many basic hues, and you can buy more of the color you choose simply by knowing the formula number. The match will be good, although perhaps not perfect (see below).

If you're trying to match paint color to the color of upholstery fabric or wallpaper, by all means take a sizable swatch of the fabric or paper with you when you go to buy the paint.

Keep in mind that factors such as the lighting in a room—whether it's fluorescent or incandescent, as well as the intensity and direction of natural light—affect the color of paint as it will look on the wall. Just as fluorescent light tends to "drain" the complexion of color, so will it cool the color of a painted surface. Incandescent light is warmer—yellows will seem more intensely yellow and blues will seem somewhat less cool if lit by standard bulbs. A pink-tinted bulb will nudge blue over in the direction of purple or lavender and make reds and pinks all the more intense. Even the color of a lampshade can work subtle but noticeable changes.

Natural light that floods in from windows with a northern exposure has little effect on color. Eastern light makes colors appear more intense. Light from the west and south warms and reddens.

How, then, do you know for sure that the paint color that seems perfect in the store won't be a disappointment on the walls of your home? You don't. But with the advice above, you *can* make allowances for lighting. Better, you can buy a quart of the color and try it out on a sizable section of the wall. Then, if it's what you want, go ahead and buy as much as you'll need of that color. Otherwise, try out another shade.

You should also keep in mind that certain colors are more difficult to paint over than others—yellow and red being the hardest of all. If you paint one coat of blue over yellow, you may end up with a sort of off-shade of blue-green. One coat of blue over red and you may get something resembling purple. This effect can be offset by applying a primer before the first coat of finish paint. Or you could use an undercoat of pigmented shellac sealer. (The sealer is made only in white, but it can be tinted, if you wish, to approximate more closely the new paint color. Ask your paint dealer about mixing some universal color into the sealer. And don't be surprised if he knows the sealer better by the name of "stain-killer.")

Finally, the same shade and color of paint may look different when applied to different surface materials such as metal, painted wood, bare wood, plaster, gypsum board, etc. So, if your intention is to paint several different kinds of surfaces the same color, your first step must be to apply a coat of the appropriate primer to each surface. Even so, you may find that a single coat of paint applied over the primer isn't enough; the different surfaces still may not appear to be precisely the same shade. If that happens, let the first coat dry, then apply a second, and perhaps a third. The point of successive coats of paint is to bring you closer to uniformity of color.

In several places throughout this book we remind you that the color of a paint can vary from batch to batch. It's always a good idea to buy all the paint you need for a particular job at the same time. If you're buying custom-mixed paint, have it all mixed up at once. If you're buying stock colors from a dealer's shelves, check the batch number on each can to make sure they all come from the same "run." And while you're at it, buy a quart or so extra for touch-ups.

III

Rollers, Brushes, Paint Pads & Other Tools of the Trade

Just as there are dozens of different kinds of paint and other coating materials, there is an enormous variety of applicators and tools to use with them. In fact, the well-stocked paint or hardware store may have such an array of so many different tools for so many different purposes that the novice painter can scarcely help but wander the aisles in bewilderment. How *does* one know what one needs for the job?

Some clues may be offered on the labels of the paint containers you've chosen. So first of all, check those labels to find out whether the manufacturer recommends specific types of applicators for use with the paint. Don't be surprised if you don't find this kind of information on most labels, however. One paint executive tells us that as much as his company might like to do it, it is impossible to include on a label everything the customer wants to know about using his paint product. A label is just too small.

You can also query salespeople. Some can be enormously helpful. Others won't know, much less care, what tools and equipment you need to do a good job. Their primary interest is in making a sale.

In the end, it may be up to you to find out about the various tools and how and when to use them. The following guide was put together with such questions in mind.

THE INDISPENSABLE ROLLER

Time was when professional house painters (some of them, anyway) looked askance at the paint roller, use of which was considered by them to be amateurish indeed. As a result, there grew up a kind of "mystique of the brush." Only with a brush, it was said by some painters, could one get a truly smooth, artistic, professional-looking job.

"What about this artistry-of-the-brush thing?" we asked the experts at several major paint companies. "Is it true that you can't get first-rate results when you apply paint with a roller?" Each expert answered in basically the same way: A roller, provided it's the right kind for the job, is an excellent and speedy way to paint.

Then whence the prejudice against rollers? Well, they told us, for a long time many union painters didn't want to use rollers precisely because rollers *are* so speedy. As payment was made on an hourly basis, the more time it took a painter to complete a job, the more money he got for it. That a roller is an inferior painting tool is simply a spurious excuse for not using one.

That's mostly in the past. These days, rollers are routinely used by professional and amateur painters alike. Most experts agree that for painting any large, flat surface—and many smaller flat and even curved surfaces—a roller is best.

HOW TO CHOOSE THE BEST ROLLER
FOR THE JOB

There are two main parts to a roller: the handle and the cover. The cover is the cylindrical part that actually applies the paint to a surface, as you roll it.

The handle should be designed so that the cover can be slipped on and off easily. (You'll need to remove the cover to clean it; there will also be times when you'll want to replace it with a new one.) The grip end of the handle should be threaded so that an extension pole can be screwed in. That way, you can use the roller for painting ceilings and the farthest reaches of your walls.

In many stores, the complete roller—handle and cover—is sold as a package. For certain painting jobs, however, you'll need special roller covers, and these can be bought separately.

You can purchase rollers in a number of different sizes, from a whopping fourteen inches wide to a diminutive one or two inches. Roller covers are available with naps that range from very flat and smooth to a deep 1¼-inch pile. Most covers are made of synthetic fiber or of lambskin or mohair.

How do you know what kind of roller you'll need for a particular job? Keep the following two general guidelines in mind when you shop for one:

1. *The larger the surface you're planning to paint, the wider should be the roller.*

There are a couple of good reasons for using a wide roller to paint large, flat surfaces. Both reasons have to do with speed. For one thing, a wide roller covers more territory per stroke than a narrow one; thus, the work gets finished faster. For another, a wide roller helps prevent unsightly lap marks (the lines of demarcation that show where applications of paint stop and start). Lap marks can be a problem when a freshly painted section begins to dry before adjacent sections have been painted—which can happen when you're using a quick-drying latex paint of dubious quality and a too-narrow roller is slowing your progress.

More specifics about roller widths:

- A 7- or 9-inch-wide roller is your best choice for painting ceilings and walls that are reasonably free of large bumps and indentations. (You may have to switch to a narrower roller, or a brush, for wall areas that bulge or are uneven because of structural irregularities or bad plastering; a wide roller would bridge the uneven areas and fail to cover them.)

- A 14-inch-wide roller covers even more area per stroke, but it's unwieldy and may take a bit of getting used to. Many pros prefer to save these giant-size rollers for the very biggest jobs.

- A 2-inch-wide trim roller makes short work of painting doorframes and window sashes as well as many other trim surfaces. This size can also be used to paint furniture. (Also available are 1- and 3-inch trim rollers.)

- A beveled, doughnut-shaped corner roller will help you roll paint right into corners, and into the angles where wall meets wall, or wall meets ceiling (assuming of course that adjacent surfaces are to be covered with the same paint). It can also be used to paint the grooves in moldings and panels.

The second rule has to do with the cover. It goes this way:

2. *The rougher the surface to be painted, the longer should be the nap or pile of the cover.*

A roller cover with a dense, deep pile works best when you're painting brick, stamped tin, or other surfaces that are heavily textured, bumpy, or uneven. Deep pile fibers can reach into and coat all the big and little irregularities of these surfaces. A deep pile cover also picks up and distributes more paint than a shorter-napped one, which means you don't have to stop and reload it as often.

However, a deep pile roller tends to leave in its wake some irregularities of its own—a kind of light dimpled, rippled pattern. This pattern may be unobjectionable and even unnoticeable when you're painting surfaces that are less than perfectly smooth. But when you want a texture-free, high-gloss finish, your best bet is a very short-napped roller.

Most painting jobs require roller covers that are somewhere in between.

- For applying flat- or satin-finish latex paint to reasonably smooth walls and ceilings—which is the kind of painting most of us do most often—choose a roller cover with a nap that is ⅜ to ½ inch deep.

- For painting heavily textured surfaces, choose a roller cover with a nap that is ¾ inch deep or more. Deep pile of 1 inch to 1¼ inches is useful for painting brick walls, stucco, etc.

- For applying high-gloss enamel or varnish, choose a roller cover with a very flat, short nap of ⅜ inch or less.

Keep in mind that many experts prefer synthetic-fiber roller covers for applying latex paints. Synthetics such as nylon, rayon, and a few others may be used. Rayon covers are the cheapest, but they're almost always a poor choice, since rayon neither spreads the paint nor holds up as well during painting as the others. Synthetic-fiber roller covers may also be used to apply alkyd paints, and many pros prefer them although lamb's-wool roller covers also may be used with alkyds. Mohair rollers have the finest, shortest nap of all and are a good choice when you want to achieve a glassy smooth enamel finish.

There are also a few specialty roller covers on the market. For acoustical ceilings there are foam roller covers patterned in grooves. For a textured effect, you can use a—what else?—texture roller. (But a texture roller is not the best choice for applying texture paint. Confusing? For how to work with texture paints, see page 99.)

WHY YOU SHOULD CHOOSE GOOD QUALITY ROLLERS—AND HOW TO KNOW THEM WHEN YOU SEE THEM

Picture a cat that's just come in out of the rain, its fur all matted and splayed. That's pretty much how a poor-quality roller cover begins to look about halfway through painting a medium-size room: matted, splayed, and next to impossible to paint with. When a roller cover gets into that condition, the paint is laid on unevenly. Great globs of it are applied in some places, while other areas are skipped. You have to go back over and over again to smooth it out. Even then, the end result may leave much to be desired.

The poor-quality handle may be less of a problem. But if it allows the roller to spin too easily, the paint will spatter. And if it resists turning, the paint will be dragged across the surface rather than spread on smoothly and evenly.

Better to spend a little more money and get a roller that enables you to do a good, fast job—even if you plan to throw that roller out when you're finished. Better still, *don't* throw it out. With proper care, a good roller cover can be used many, many times, while a good handle can be fitted with a variety of different kinds of covers—two factors that make a good quality roller a much better bargain than a cheap one if you plan to do much of your own painting.

How do you know that the roller you're buying is a good one? When brand new, a good roller and a poor-quality one may look very much the same. To the amateur painter, their respective price tags may be the most obvious difference between them. The truth is, cost *is* an indication of quality. Though it won't always be true that the *most* expensive roller is the best one, you can be sure that the roller priced very much below all the others is no bargain. You can also be guided by some of the following points:

- The nap or pile of a good roller is dense and springy.

- The tube inside a good quality roller cover is metal or plastic, or cardboard on metal or plastic—not plain cardboard or paper.

- The handle of a good roller is designed so that the cover can be easily slipped on and off. Cheaper handles often have wing nuts which must be unscrewed in order to remove or replace a cover.

- The handle should be made so that it can be used with an extension pole.

- Handles with plastic grips are preferred by many pros. That's because so much painting now is done with latex paint, which requires water for cleanup, and all that water might ultimately damage a wooden handle.

ROLLER TRAYS AND GRIDS

You can hardly use a roller without a roller tray from which to load it. If you don't already have a tray, buy one when you get the roller.

Many painters also like to use a roller-tray grid. These grids, made of heavily perforated plastic or metal, fit along the sloped surface of the roller tray. A grid makes it easier to do a proper job of loading the roller; excess paint is removed when the roller is drawn up the length of the grid.

You can buy disposable plastic roller-tray liners that fit the bottom of the tray and minimize tray cleanup. (Instead of cleaning the tray, just throw out the liner.) Some painters use a layer of heavy aluminum foil as a liner. If you want to improvise a foil liner, you really should have a grid to help roll off excess paint.

BASIC TECHNIQUES FOR USING
A ROLLER

1. *Before you begin*: Roller covers need to be "primed." This is just a simple matter of thoroughly wetting the cover—with water, if you're using latex paint; or with mineral spirits (paint thinner), if you're using an alkyd paint. Be sure to work water or paint thinner down into the very depths of the pile or nap. Then use paper toweling or a clean cloth to blot up the excess. The roller cover should be damp, not dripping wet.

Next, fill the roller tray with paint. Two-thirds full is about right. If the paint you are using needs to be stirred (check the label to make sure), stir it up in the can (see "boxing," page 25). Never mix paint directly in the tray.

2. *To load the roller*: Don't just dip the roller into the paint. Instead, roll it back and forth in the tray so that the entire roller cover, not just the outer pile or nap, is completely saturated. The more paint the roller picks up each time you load it, the less often you will need to go back and reload.

Now, draw the roller up the slope of the tray to remove excess paint. If paint drips off the roller when you lift it from the tray, it is overloaded. Run it back up the slope of the tray.

NOTE: The roller tray should be placed close to where you are painting. For obvious reasons, you don't want to have to carry a loaded roller any farther than is necessary.

3. *To apply the paint*: Start by rolling out a rather large, spread-out M.

The first roller stroke of the M should be *upward* if you're painting a wall. If you're painting a ceiling, the first stroke should be *away* from you; this is important. Since the roller is now fully loaded with paint, if your first stroke were a down stroke, paint

47

would accumulate just in front of the roller and would probably dribble down toward the floor. The second stroke of the M should be a down stroke (*toward* you if you're painting a ceiling). The third stroke is an up stroke; the fourth, down.

This M and the area just around it will be your first working section. Always work in sections small enough—3 feet by 3 feet is a good size—so that you don't have to stretch or bend too far in any direction to paint it out. (It's hardly ever a good idea to paint in long vertical or horizontal stripes.)

Now, fill in the section by rolling back and forth and up and down across the M.

"Feather" the paint at the boundaries of the section by using gradually lighter roller pressure as you approach the edges. Stop the roller just before lifting it off the surface. By now, the paint in the roller cover should be almost depleted. If necessary—and it almost always is—go back and with light strokes smooth out any roller marks or uneven coverage.

NOTE: Use light pressure on the first couple of strokes of the M when the roller is fully loaded. Too much pressure at first will release too much paint and you'll have to spend more time smoothing it out. As paint is released from the roller, gradually increase the pressure of your strokes. Go back to light pressure for feathering and smoothing.

Don't make the mistake of trying to "stretch" the supply of paint in the roller by bearing down hard and squeezing out every last drop it holds. Though you can finish off a section, feather it, and smooth it out with an almost-dry roller, you need a generous flow of paint at the beginning to fill in that section. If you don't get that flow, you're either (1) not loading the roller with enough paint, or (2) working in sections that are too large. Either way, adjustments are in order.

NOTE: Don't try to paint so quickly that the roller spins a spray of paint onto areas where you don't want it. That doesn't mean that you must work at a snail's pace. It does mean that there's a limit to how fast you can roll on paint. You'll quickly be able to gauge what the limit is.

4. *Now it's time to reload the roller and start a new section*: Begin this new section the way you did the first one, by rolling out another large M. The M should be near to but not butting up against the section you've just finished painting. Fill in the new section by rolling back and forth and up and down across the M. Blend the two sections by feathering the edge of the new one into the feathered edge of the previously painted section. Feather the other edges of the new section. Then with light, long, even strokes, smooth out any roller marks or uneven coverage. Finally, to avoid lap marks between sections, roll lightly over the area where they meet.

NOTE: Almost every pro we spoke with warned against stopping in the middle of painting a wall or ceiling or other large, unbroken surface area. Paint starts drying quickly. Uneven coverage and lap marks may be the result of trying to feather wet paint into paint that has already begun to dry. If you must take a break, hold out until you've completed the entire wall, ceiling, or whatever.

NOTE: The paint on your tools will dry quickly, too—so quickly that by the time you've finished eating lunch or making phone calls, etc., the paint may have hardened to the point where the roller needs a thorough cleaning before it's fit to use again. So, before you walk off the job for any length of time, take the precaution of immersing the roller in water, if you're using latex paint, or in mineral spirits, if you're using an alkyd. (Or, if you are working with alkyd paint, you could wrap the roller tightly in clear plastic wrap.) Before using the roller again, run it over newspaper, then use paper toweling to blot up as much moisture as possible.

HOW TO CLEAN AND CARE FOR ROLLERS

A roller is cleaned according to what kind of paint you've been using. The "solvent" for cleaning tools used with latex paints is water, of course. The solvents for tools used with alkyd paints are mineral spirits or turpentine.

When using mineral spirits or turpentine, remember that they are highly flammable. Work only in a well-ventilated room with the window(s) open. Don't smoke, and don't allow anyone else carrying a lighted cigarette into the room with you. For heaven's sake, don't use either solvent in the kitchen unless the pilot light of your stove has been extinguished.

Regardless of what you use to clean a roller, one important piece of advice is the same: Clean up immediately after a job is finished. The longer you wait, the harder the paint will dry on the roller, and the more difficult it will be to remove.

1. *To clean a roller used with latex paint*: First, remove as much paint as possible by running the roller back and forth over newspaper. Slip the cover off the handle and hold it under running water, gently squeezing water through the nap or pile. One old pro tells us that he puts the roller tray under the faucet in the bathtub, turns on the water, and runs the roller back and forth over the tray to clean both at the same time.

When the water runs clear (it takes a while), lather up some soap and work suds into the nap or pile. You can clean the handle with soap and water now, too.

Thoroughly rinse suds from the cover. Squeeze out as much water as you can. (Be gentle; don't wring or twist the cover out of shape.) Blot with paper toweling or an old towel. Then stand it on its end to dry. When dry, wrap the cover in plastic wrap or aluminum foil and store it away someplace—on its end, so the nap doesn't get flattened—until next time you need it.

2. *To clean a roller used with alkyd paint*: The first step is again to remove as much paint as possible by running the roller over old newspaper. Slip the cover off the handle, then saturate it with mineral spirits. One way to do this is to pour some of the solvent into the roller tray. (Empty the paint from the tray first,

of course, and wipe it out as best you can with newspaper or paper toweling.)

Work the solvent down into the nap or pile, then squeeze as much solvent as possible from the cover. By now, the solvent is saturated with paint. Switch to fresh solvent and repeat the process. You may need to use three or four batches of solvent. When it finally runs clear as you squeeze it from the cover, the cover is clean.

At this point, some pros would just blot the cover, set it on end to dry, then wrap it for storage in plastic or aluminum foil. Others say it's better to give the cover a soap and water washing followed by a thorough rinsing, before drying and wrapping for storage. Either way, when you store the cover, stand it on its end to prevent the nap from being flattened.

NOTE: Follow the procedure above when cleaning rollers used with varnish and shellac. In the case of shellac, however, clean with denatured alcohol instead of mineral spirits.

PAINTBRUSHES: THE CLASSIC APPLICATORS

Although there's a roller cover available now for almost every conceivable kind of paint job, some people still prefer to work with a brush. ("There's something very satisfying about the slap, slap, slap of a brush," says one.)

You can't cover as much territory as quickly with a brush as you can with a roller, but what is lost in speed may be made up for in control, which is one reason why many people feel more comfortable with a brush.

How to Choose the Right Brush for the Job

You don't have to know everything there is to know about paintbrushes when you go out to buy one, but you should know

51

that some brushes are better for particular jobs than others, and why.

1. *Bristles are a factor.* Brushes you'll find in stores today are made either with natural bristles (from animals) or synthetic bristles (made of man-made fibers such as nylon). Actually, you'll probably find a much larger selection of synthetic-bristle brushes than of the natural bristle kind, and that's not bad. Although it used to be that the only good brush was a natural-bristle brush, the quality new synthetic brushes offer results that are every bit as good. And they'll cost you less, too.

If cost were no object, and you wanted to decide between natural and synthetic bristles, which should be your choice? It depends.

- Synthetic bristles are best if you're going to be using a latex paint or any material that uses water for cleanup. Natural bristles are highly water absorbent, which makes them incompatible for use with latex paints.

- If you're using an alkyd paint or other oil-base coating, you can choose either synthetic or natural bristles.

Whether bristles are synthetic or natural, the earmarks of a good quality brush—the kind that picks up and applies paint with maximum smoothness and ease—are the same. Here are some of them:

- Bristles on a quality brush are thick, flexible, and springy— not silky fine and limp, not stubby and rigid. Draw the bristles across your hand. Individual bristles should conform to the contours, then immediately spring back into shape. As you make this little test, watch to see whether individual bristles flex more at their tip ends, or at the base of the brush where they're attached. Good bristles have their greatest flexibility at the *tips*. Separate the bristles and

52

check to see that there are no bald, empty spots at the center of the brush.

- Bristle length has a lot to do with flexibility. Too-long bristles may have a floppy quality and do a sloppy job. Trying to apply paint with bristles that are too short is like trying to paint with a scrub brush. An often-quoted rule of thumb is that bristles should be half again as long as the brush is wide.

- Bristle tips should be "flagged" or split at the ends (something like a split hair). Flagged bristles pick up more paint and apply it more smoothly.

- Bristles should be "staggered" in length. To see whether they are, draw the brush across the palm of your hand and watch to see if there are shorter bristles that spring back before longer ones.

You'll undoubtedly find many brushes in a store that have few or none of the desirable features just mentioned. These brushes will cost less than the others and you may be tempted to buy one with the intention of throwing it out when the paint job is completed. Don't.

A poor-quality brush won't be fit to paint with in a very short while—probably well before you've finished the work in progress. It will also slow you down and make the job harder from the start.

A cheap brush made with blunt rather than flagged bristles will pick up less paint. Because of the way it's made, paint will tend to drizzle off as you carry it to the surface to be painted. Once there, the paint won't flow off as smoothly as it would from a good brush, and you'll have to do more in order to get rid of brush marks. Most frustrating of all, cheap brushes tend to shed a trail of bristles in their wake—which means you'll be spending time picking them off and smoothing over the places where they were embedded. That way lies madness.

2. *As for brush size*: The general principle is the same as it is for rollers, and for the same reason—a wider brush covers more territory faster than a narrow one. So, the larger the surface you're planning to paint, the wider should be the brush that you use. It's a rule so obvious as to seem almost not worth mentioning. But we do mention it because not one, but several paint-supply salespeople told us that their customers are inclined to choose brushes that are too narrow for good, fast painting.

"Why would they do that?" we asked. Well, according to a salesman in a giant New York City paint outlet, part of the reason has to do with wanting to save money. A narrow brush, obviously, is less expensive than a wider brush of comparable quality. But there's also the fact that some of the wider brushes are too wide to be dipped into a quart-size paint can. In other words, some people buy a narrower brush so that they can load it directly from the paint can.

If money is a critical factor, then you may indeed be better off with a good-quality brush that is somewhat too narrow for maximum convenience and speed than with a wider brush of poor quality.

But don't choose a narrower brush simply because it fits inside a paint can. Instead, do what many professionals do: When you're ready to start a job, transfer paint from the can you bought it in to a clean, dry bucket or pail and load the brush from that. You *could* use the same bucket you use for scrubbing the kitchen floor. But keep in mind that most paint stores carry very inexpensive disposable buckets that are handy for "boxing" anyway and that save you the trouble of cleanup; just throw them out when you're finished.

Another good reason to transfer paint from can to bucket is to keep the groove around the rim of the can from filling up with paint, which it always does when you load a brush directly from the can. If that groove is filled with paint when you put the lid back on the can, you're going to have trouble getting the lid off again when you need to. (If all of this has convinced you to work from a bucket instead of a paint can, don't pour the paint from can to bucket, or paint will run into the groove. Instead, ladle the paint with a paper cup.)

Just how wide is a brush that's wide enough for a particular job? Wall brushes—the kind to use on walls and ceilings—come in widths ranging from 3 inches to 7 inches. The best width will depend to some degree on your own strength and endurance. The 7-inch brush will of course paint a wider swath in one stroke than the 3-incher. But it's heavy! And it will seem to get heavier as the job progresses. The 3-inch size is a little skimpy, but if your arm tires very easily it may be best for you. If you're reasonably robust, a 4-inch or 5-inch brush is a good choice.

Any fairly well-stocked store where paint and paint supplies are sold will have on display a number of brushes in a great many widths and even many shapes. You won't need one of each. If your goal is to paint an average room, you'll need a collection of two or possibly three brushes. They are:

A wall brush.

A trim brush, 1 or 2 inches wide, to get at all the hard-to-reach places that are too small to paint with a wall brush.

An angled sash brush, perhaps. Narrower than a wall brush, the sash brush can be used flat or on its angled edge for cutting in close on narrow surfaces where precision is called for—such as where window sash meets glass, doorframe meets wall, etc.

Basic Techniques for Using a Paintbrush

1. *Before you begin*: Don't be alarmed if you've paid good money for a high-quality brush and you notice a *few* loose bristles. Most new brushes will have a few strays. Once the strays are removed, you should have very little more shedding. To get rid of loose bristles, gently ruffle the bristle ends by running your fingers back and forth through the tips. Then shake the brush or tap it hard against the palm of your hand. Do this a few times and you're ready to "prime" the brush for painting.

To prime a brush that will be used with latex paint, wet the bristles with water, then blot up the excess with paper toweling or a clean, dry cloth. Bristles should be damp through and through, but not dripping. To prime a brush that will be used with oil-base paint, saturate the bristles with paint thinner and wipe away excess. Again, the bristles should be damp, but not dripping.

2. *To load the brush*: Dip brush into the paint to about halfway up the length of the bristles. Do this several times. The idea is to thoroughly saturate the bristles. Dip again, this time gently stirring the paint with the brush. (This stirring motion tends to "open" or spread the bristles so that they'll take up more paint. However, it's not a good idea to go on stirring paint in this way each time the brush is loaded.)

Remove the loaded brush from the paint container by lifting it straight up and pausing a moment to allow any drips to drop back into the container. To release excess paint from the brush, tap it gently against the inside rim of the container.

NOTE: All the pros we talked with say it's bad form to try to remove excess paint by wiping the bristles across the top edge of the container. This way of doing it tends to make the bristles clump up and causes brush marks on the surface that will take extra time to smooth. (Also, if you're painting straight from the can, wiping the brush across the top will cause paint to collect in the groove.)

NOTE: Never dip your brush to a depth of more than halfway up the bristles. The main reason for this no-no has to do with avoiding an accumulation of paint at the base of the bristles— up near the handle, or "heel," of the brush. You don't get much mileage out of paint that far up on the brush; the fastest, smoothest work is done with the tip half of the bristles. Paint in the heel tends to drip down onto your hand if you're working above shoulder level. Paint in the heel also makes the job of cleaning the brush that much more difficult.

3. *To apply the paint*: Always work in sections. Most people find that when they are painting ceilings or walls, sections of approximately 3 feet by 3 feet are convenient and manageable.

Begin by placing four or five slaps or dabs of paint on the surface. Use one side of the brush for the first couple of dabs, the other side for the final dabs. Since the brush is now fully loaded, you won't need to exert much pressure to lay on a generous amount of paint with each dab.

Now, brush out the section so that the dabs are blended together. Use short diagonal up-and-down strokes (accomplished by a quick flexing of the wrist), so that with each stroke an alternating side of the brush slaps the surface. (That slap, slap sound *can* be very satisfying, but don't get *too* slaphappy or you'll end up with paint spatters everywhere.) Another way to brush out the section is to use quick, firm crescent or half-moon-shaped strokes.

Next, feather the edges of the section. In feathering, you gradually reduce the pressure of the strokes as you approach the edge of a section, until you are painting with only the very tip ends of the bristles. Feathering at the edges isn't meant to result in complete coverage, but instead produces a feathery-looking pattern—just as the name implies. The purpose of feathering is to avoid a too-thick coating where one painted section meets another.

Finally, even out any brush marks by smoothing the section with long, light strokes, using just the tip ends of the bristles.

NOTE: Some pros like to have these long, even finishing strokes running all in one direction—usually straight up and down. Others say it's better to have finishing strokes going off in all different directions so that if any brush marks remain they will be less noticeable because they follow no discernible pattern. Still others make it a practice to have finishing strokes on smooth surfaces going in one direction only, but vary the direction of finishing strokes on rough surfaces. That way, they say, all irregularities on a rough surface are sure to be covered. Everyone agrees that finishing strokes on wood surfaces should follow the grain of the wood.

NOTE: Always work the paint outward, toward the edges of a section, rather than inward toward the center. Otherwise you may end with a pileup of paint at the center.

NOTE: There is no one best way to hold a paintbrush. Some people use a modified pencil-grip. Others like a tennis-racquet grip, or prefer to have a thumb resting on top of the handle while they support the weight of the handle in the palm of their hand. Still others control a brush in what might almost be described as "chopstick" style. What really matters is that the brush should feel comfortable and natural. Your grip should be firm, of course, but there's no point in clutching that brush for dear life. A too-tight grip won't help you paint better; in fact, it may actually hinder you, since your arm may tire more quickly.

NOTE: Even the best of brushes may shed an occasional hair. Should one get stuck on the surface you're painting, you can remove it simply by touching it with the tip end of the wet brush. Wipe it off the brush with a clean cloth or paper toweling.

By the time you've feathered the edges of a section and smoothed away brush marks, your brush should need reloading. Then you'll be ready to paint a new section adjacent to the just-painted one.

4. *Start the new section as you did the old one*: Apply four or five dabs of paint near to, but not touching, the just-painted section. Then use diagonal up-and-down or crescent-shaped strokes to spread paint over the entire new section. Feather the edges into the feathered edges of the old section and smooth away brush marks with long, light-pressure strokes with the tips of the bristles.

Continue working in sections until you've completed the job.

NOTE: Should you have to leave a partially painted wall or ceiling for more than a few minutes, you can prevent paint from drying on your brush by immersing it in water (if you're using latex paint) or mineral spirits (if you're using an alkyd paint).

How to Clean and Care for Brushes

The same advice applies to cleaning brushes as to cleaning rollers: Do it as soon as possible after you've finished a job. Remember, paint dries quickly. And dried paint is much more difficult to clean off than paint that's still in its wet state.

1. *To clean a brush used with latex paint*: Hold the brush under a lukewarm stream from the faucet. Gently separate the bristles so that interior bristles down at the base get a good bath. When the water runs clear, fill the sink or other container with warm water and mild soap suds and allow the brush to soak for a minute or two. Then swish suds through the brush, paying special attention to the bristles at the base. Thoroughly rinse brush in clear water. Blot with a paper towel or clean cloth. (Be careful not to twist or bend the bristles.)

At this point, some pros like to straighten and smooth the bristles by combing through them with a fine-tooth comb or special brush made for this purpose. Others simply hang the brush up to dry. (If you can't easily devise a way to hang the brush, allow it to dry on its side on a flat surface. Wet or dry, never stand a brush on its bristles.)

When the brush is dry, wrap it in paper or aluminum foil and store.

2. *To clean a brush used with oil-base paint*: Pour paint thinner or turpentine into a container and allow the brush to soak in it for a few minutes. As it soaks, separate and flex the bristles back and forth so that the solvent can penetrate through to the interior bristles. With your hands, work the solvent through the bristles at the base of the brush. Use a paint scraper or similar tool to loosen and remove hardened-on deposits of paint on the bristle end of the handle.

Switch to fresh solvent and repeat the process. You may need to repeat with fresh solvent several times. When paint no longer colors the solvent, the brush is clean.

59

If your brush is made of natural bristles, remove excess solvent by shaking the brush a couple of times and blotting it with paper toweling. If you like, run a fine-tooth comb through the bristles to smooth and straighten them. Then hang the brush to dry, or allow it to dry on its side on a flat surface. When it's completely dry, wrap the brush in paper or aluminum foil and store it either hanging or on a flat surface.

If your brush is made with synthetic bristles, you might want to follow up solvent cleaning with a quick dunk in lukewarm sudsy water. Rinse thoroughly. Blot. Then allow to dry as above.

NEWFANGLED APPLICATORS: PAINT PADS AND OTHERS

Within the last few years a number of ingenious paint applicators have been developed to challenge the efficiency and popularity of rollers and brushes. Probably the best known and most serious contender for the title of "most efficient applicator" is the paint pad.

A paint pad is just that—a pad, often of nylon or mohair, sometimes of foam, which is attached to a frame and handle and used to "wipe" paint onto a surface.

Paint pads, like rollers and brushes, come in a range of sizes and shapes suited to various kinds of jobs. Very wide 8-inch pads make quick work of walls and ceilings. (Some handles are threaded to take an extension pole, which makes them extra-convenient for doing ceilings and painting high up on walls.) Smaller pads can be had in just the right sizes for painting different trim surfaces. Wedge-shaped pads can be used to apply paint neatly and cleanly into corners.

There are pads of varying fiber lengths for painting different surface textures. Pads with short fibers are for smooth surfaces. Those with longer fibers are for painting textured surfaces such as stucco and brick.

Pros who have used all three kinds of applicators are in general agreement that painting with a pad is faster than painting with a brush, but not quite as fast as using a roller. However, because of the way they're made, pads spatter and drip less than rollers *or* brushes. And one pro particularly likes pads because they leave less texture on the surface than other applicators. Which means there's also less going back to smooth the surface once the paint has been laid on.

Basic Techniques for Using Paint Pads

1. *Before you begin*: Wet the pad with water, if you're using latex paint, or with mineral spirits, if you're using an alkyd paint. Make sure the pad is dampened through and through. Then blot with a cloth.

2. *To load the pad*: You'll need a roller tray or a rather large, shallow pan. If you use a roller tray, fill it up with paint about two thirds of the way. Then, being careful not to allow paint to soak into the foam backing under the fibers of the pad, draw the pad up the slope of the roller tray. Some of the paint will come along with it. Rock the pad back and forth in the paint on the slope, then lift it straight up, pausing to allow excess paint to drip off. Now the pad is loaded and ready to go.

If you use a pan, first pour in some paint, then immerse the pad's fibers only. In other words, don't dip the pad so deeply into the paint that the foam backing becomes saturated. Lift the pad straight up out of the pan. Pause to allow excess paint to drip off, or wipe the pad gently against the edge of the pan.

There are a couple of rather new gadgets on the market that make paint-pad loading easier still. One is a special roller tray fitted with a wheel-like cylindrical device that picks up paint as it revolves in the tray. To load the pad, fill the tray with paint, then run the pad back and forth over the cylinder. It's hard to overload the pad with this gadget, and there's little danger of paint soaking into the pad's foam backing. Newer still is a cylindrical "dispenser" that can be clipped onto *any* roller tray. With

this, the procedure is again to fill the tray with paint, then run
the pad back and forth over the cylinder.

NOTE: The pad should be loaded with a generous amount
of paint, but not so much that the pressure of applying it to a
surface causes the paint to gush out and down the wall.

3. *To apply the paint*: Work in sections of approximately
3 feet by 3 feet.

With gentle pressure, wipe paint on in the shape of an M.
Fill in the section by lightly wiping in one-way strokes across
the M. Feather the edges of the section as you approach them
by gradually decreasing presure on the pad and lifting it from
the surface.

NOTE: Wipe the pad smoothly across the surface. Don't scrub
or rub back and forth. When the pad begins to drag or pull hard
against the surface, it needs reloading. Certainly it will need to
be reloaded by the time you've finished painting a 3-foot-square
section.

Start new sections near to but not butting up against the
feathered edges of the section just painted. Begin with an M.
Fill in by wiping in one-way strokes across the M. Then feather
the edges into the feathered edges of the old section.

Continue painting in sections until you've finished the job.

How to Clean Paint Pads

Assuming you're not using one of the popular disposable
pads (in which case, simply detach it from the frame and get rid
of it), your first step in cleaning a pad is to use paper toweling
or newspaper to blot up and wipe away excess paint. Next, separate pad from frame.

1. *If you've been using latex paint*: Work lukewarm water
through the fibers of the pad. When the water runs clear or almost
clear, dunk the pad in sudsy water. Rinse thoroughly. Blot. Then

set it out on a clean, flat surface to dry. If necessary, use soap and water to clean frame and handle.

2. *To clean a pad used with oil-base paint*: Immerse it in paint thinner that has been poured into a pan or other container. Work the thinner through the fibers of the pad. Then repeat with fresh thinner. The pad is clean when paint no longer colors fresh thinner. (You may have to go through three or four batches of thinner before the pad comes clean.) Squeeze excess thinner from the pad, then blot with a paper towel or clean cloth. Set the pad on a flat, clean surface to dry. If necessary, use paint thinner to clean frame and handle.

It's always a good idea to store the pad wrapped in paper or aluminum foil. That way it will be clean and ready to go next time you want to use it.

PAINT MITTS: HOW AND WHEN
TO USE THEM

Ever wonder what those fuzzy or woolly-looking mitts you see in paint and hardware stores are all about? Well, they're used to apply paint. Just slip one on, dip it in some paint, then wipe it across the surface you want painted.

No one we talked with took the paint mitt very seriously. Or at least no one cared to recommend it for general painting use. This is partly because with the paint mitt your arm functions as a handle, which can get to be very tiring indeed. However, some pros thought a mitt was just dandy for applying paint to oddly bent or curved surfaces such as the pipes you run into in some kitchens and bathrooms (and the walls behind them), radiators, balustrades, balusters, etc. In other words, because of its flexibility, a mitt might be a timesaver when you want to paint something that you can easily wrap your hand—but not a brush, roller, or pad—around.

There are no established techniques for using a mitt. Just be sure you don't overload it. (After dipping it into the paint, wipe off the excess on the edge of the container.) Then spread the paint on as best you can.

To clean a paint mitt used with latex paint, hold it under a flow of lukewarm water. You might find that it's easiest to do this when you're wearing the mitt. Work the water through the pile. When the water runs clear, wash the mitt in lukewarm suds. Rinse thoroughly. Shake off excess water. Blot. Then allow to dry.

To clean a mitt used with oil-base paint, work paint thinner through the pile. Continue until fresh thinner runs clear. Shake off excess thinner. Blot. Then allow the mitt to dry.

SPRAY GUNS: FOR PROS ONLY?

A spray gun is no novelty item. For years now professionals have relied on the spray gun for painting very large surfaces. In fact, there's nothing quite like a spray gun for getting big jobs (factories, warehouses, new-apartment-building interiors) over and done with in record time.

But what if you're the average amateur painter of an occasional wall or ceiling? Would it be worth your while to invest in and master the techniques of spray-painting with a gun?

Probably not. Setting up for spray-painting (getting yourself, your supplies and equipment, and the surfaces you *don't* want painted ready for the job) is more time-consuming than setting up for other kinds of painting. Spray-painting is potentially more dangerous; the techniques can be tricky; and the results, though they may be good, are probably no better than the results achieved by other methods.

However, if you already own a spray gun, or know someone who'd be happy to lend you one—or if you're just plain curious enough about spray-painting with a gun to want to buy or rent an outfit, the following guidelines for how to use it may come in handy.

1. *Before you begin*: Read and make sure you have a thorough understanding of the instructions for use that come with the spray gun. Take special note of suggested safety precautions.

Fill the gun with *water* to practice. The tiled back wall of a tub or shower would be a good target for practice-painting with water. Better still, practice by "shooting" the gun at an exterior wall.

- Hold the gun in an upright position 8 to 10 inches from the "target" surface. Assuming you're practicing on a large surface, plan to make each horizontal stroke or pass with the gun approximately 3 feet long.

- Practice starting each pass slightly *ahead* of the target. Pull the trigger the instant before the nozzle is lined up with the edge of the target. Move your arm in a straight line parallel to the target. Release the trigger at the other edge of the target area, but continue the pass slightly beyond it. Now, move the gun back in a return pass.

- Ideally, the paint sprayed on with each successive pass should overlap by about 50 percent the paint sprayed on with the previous pass.

- It's important to keep each stroke or pass parallel to the target surface. It's the only way to get a smooth, even coating. The closer the gun is held to the surface, the heavier will be the paint coverage; the farther the gun is from the surface, the lighter will be the coverage. With that in mind, it's easy to see how arcing swings or any passes at the surface that are *not* parallel to it would result in uneven coverage.

- Move the gun past the surface at a uniform speed. Obviously, the slower you move the gun, the heavier will be the coverage, and vice versa. If you pause over some areas and move very rapidly over others, the coverage will be uneven.

Keep practicing until you have a good feel for the capabilities of the gun and for your own ability to work with it.

2. *When it's time to paint*: Mask (with tape), cover (with drop cloths, newspaper, or both), or move out of the way all furniture, rugs or anything else that you don't want painted. That way, there'll be no real damage done if your aim is faulty at first, or the spray gun happens to misfire.

If you're going to be spray-painting a piece of furniture—a chair, for example, or a chest—you might want to improvise a spraying "booth." Scout around for a cardboard carton large enough to enclose the object you're painting. Remove the top flaps, stand the carton on its side, then place chest, chair, or whatever in the carton. Now you can spray without fear of painting your walls and floors as well; the sides and back of the "booth" will catch any overspray.

Make sure there is good ventilation in the area where you'll be working. Keep at least one window or door open (more if possible). But if there's a stiff breeze blowing through that window, close it and open another one with a different exposure. Wind can easily blow a mist of paint right past its target—and even back onto you. (Obviously, trying to do spray-painting outdoors on a windy day won't work.)

Don't spray paint in the kitchen or any area where there is an open flame. Keep all smokers out of the area as well.

Protect your hair with a hat or scarf, wear gloves, and, just before you begin to paint, tie a handkerchief loosely over your nose and mouth so that you don't accidentally inhale any spray.

Stir and/or dilute the paint you are going to use according to the instructions on the label. Strain off any lumps, bumps, or foreign particles that might clog the nozzle of the gun by pouring the paint through fine cheesecloth or an old nylon stocking.

Follow the manufacturer's instructions for loading the gun.

3. *To apply the paint*: Use the techniques suggested for practice-painting with water: Make parallel three-feet-wide passes at the target. Keep the gun moving at a uniform speed back and forth across the target.

The freshly painted surface should look glossy and wet. But if just-sprayed paint begins to drip or sag, coverage is too heavy. Either move slightly away from the target, or speed up your strokes, or both. If the paint fails to cover the surface completely, put less distance between gun and target, or slow down your strokes, or both.

Remember that two or three thin coats of any paint—whether you roll, brush, wipe, or spray it on—are always better than one thick coat.

NOTE: Techniques for spraying paint or other material that comes in an aerosol can are essentially the same as for spray-painting with a gun. Just be sure to shake the can before spraying, and to pause every few minutes to shake it again. Be sure to read and follow to the letter all instructions for use printed on the aerosol can.

Cleaning the Spray Gun

Cleaning a spray gun always involves shooting through it some of the solvent appropriate to the paint you have used—water for latex paint, mineral spirits for alkyd paint, denatured alcohol for shellac, etc. When in doubt, check the paint can to see what the manufacturer recommends for cleanup. Then clean the gun according to instructions given by *its* manufacturer. (There are several different kinds of spray guns; the procedure for cleaning each is slightly different, depending on the way it is made.)

Do clean up quickly. Putting it off will only make the job harder.

OTHER CRUCIAL TOOLS
AND EQUIPMENT

There's no end to the tools and equipment you *could* buy. Go into any hardware or paint store and just look around. It seems that there's a gimmick or gadget designed for every conceivable set of painting circumstances that might arise. Some are specific problem-solvers; others simply make easier work of certain jobs. There'd be no point in listing them all here, though many are referred to in the chapters that follow when special painting techniques are dealt with.

Some tools, on the other hand, are essential to just about any painting job. If you plan to do much of your own painting, you will find yourself using them over and over and over again. Here they are:

Drop cloths.   Layers of old newspaper are just fine for protecting some surfaces, but you still need drop cloths for covering furniture and floors. Drop cloths are inexpensive. If you've never used them, you'll wonder how you ever got along without them.

A stepladder.   Even if you have an extension pole for your roller, you still need some way of getting up close to the ceiling to cut in along the edges where it meets the wall. If you're tall enough, standing on a chair might get you up as high as you need to be. But a stepladder gives you something to hang on to, and a place to put your paint. If you don't have one, get one. (You'll be happy you did the next time you have to change a light bulb in a ceiling fixture.)

Sandpaper.   You'll need it for smoothing areas that are flaking or peeling, for deglossing (more about that later on) walls and trim, and for giving "tooth" to previously painted surfaces. Common, garden variety sandpaper—medium grit—is good enough for most surfaces. For sanding furniture, buy garnet or aluminum oxide abrasive paper.

Masking tape. Often there are better ways to protect what you don't want painted, but sometimes nothing but masking tape will do. Always have some on hand.

Paint shields. These are long, flat, very thin pieces of metal or plastic used to protect various surfaces from being smeared with paint. You hold one, in one hand, against the surface you want to protect; then you paint with the other hand. Paint shields are cheap, preferable to masking tape in many situations, and available at any hardware or paint store.

Putty knife (or knives). Some putty knives have wide, flexible blades; others have narrower, less flexible blades; still others have wide, fairly rigid blades. Have one of each. They don't cost much and they'll be handy for any number of uses in addition to helping you patch an occasional crack in the wall.

IV

How to Paint Ceilings & Walls

Let's assume that you want to paint a room. You've already decided on the kind and color of paint to use on ceiling, walls, and trim. You've calculated and bought an adequate amount of all the paint and primer you'll need. In short, you're ready to begin the job. How do you proceed?

There's a standard sequence to painting a room. It goes this way:

- Ceiling

- Trim (doors and doorframes, window frames and sash, etc.)

- Masonry (brick, stone, tile) if there is any, and you intend to paint it

- Walls

If you're going to paint the floor, do it last. *However,* if you're going to completely refinish a floor, get that out of the way first. Refinishing requires sanding, and you don't want all that sawdust to ruin your fresh paint job.

The logic of the sequence is impeccable. You do the ceiling first so you don't have to worry about splashes and spatters dripping down to mar fresh paint below. You do the trim before the walls so that no great damage is done if you accidentally smear a little trim paint or enamel on a wall; just cover it up later with wall paint. If you're painting a whole room, you'll get the best results if you follow this sequence.

However, even though they *don't* follow in sequence, we're going to treat ceilings and walls together in this chapter and save trim and masonry for later on. That's because ceilings and walls are so similar. With a few exceptions and minor variations, the techniques for preparing and then painting them are the same. So are most of the problems that can arise—and the methods for heading those problems off at the beginning.

Trim is something else again. So is masonry. Each deserves a chapter of its own because the painting techniques and the materials required are so distinctly different.

NOTE: Before you paint a room, read all the chapters in this book that apply so that you'll know how to proceed and what additional tools or materials you'll need, if any. Then, when it's time to paint, refer back to specifics if necessary.

HOW TO GET READY TO PAINT
A ROOM

1. *What to wear.* Old clothes, of course. Anything you don't care about, as long as the ensemble doesn't hamper freedom of movement. Don't forget old shoes or sneakers. Cover your hair with an old scarf or hat, or improvise a paper-bag cap as some professional painters do.

Cold cream or Vaseline petroleum jelly applied to your face and other exposed skin will make it easier to get paint speckles off yourself. Don't grease up your hands or you'll have a hard time keeping a grip on paintbrush or roller.

2. *What to do about the furniture.* It would be nice if you could get everything you don't want painted out of the room so you wouldn't have to worry about paint damage to any of your possessions. And you'd also have greater maneuverability within the room.

Completely emptying out the room may very well be impractical, so at the least move whatever you can to an adjoining room. Chairs, end tables and coffee tables, lamps, throw rugs, magazine stands—anything portable should be stowed elsewhere for the duration.

As for heavy furniture that must stay in the room, where you move it first depends on whether you are going to be painting ceiling and walls, or walls only.

If painting the ceiling is on the agenda, get someone to help you move big pieces over into one corner of the room. Ceilings are done first, remember. With all of the furniture in one corner, you can paint most of the ceiling, then move everything to the center of the room to finish. The furniture stays in the center of the room while you paint the walls.

If you're doing walls only, simply move furniture to the center of the room.

3. *What to do about windows, doors, light fixtures, and objects hanging on the walls.* Take down curtains and draperies as well as blinds or shades and the contraptions by which they're hung. If any of these need cleaning, this is the time to do it. (No, not this very moment, but before you put them back up again.)

If you can do so easily, remove hardware (doorknobs, locks, and handles) from doors—even if you plan to paint these things later. With hardware removed, painting the door itself will go faster. The hardware will look better when it's back in place if you paint it separately. Hardware that's been painted all at once with the surface behind it tends to have a gunked-up, sloppy look.

What if you prefer the look of bare metal, but hardware is already painted? Place the hardware in a container along with enough paint remover to cover. By the time you're ready to replace the hardware, the coating of paint on it will be softened and easy to remove.

NOTE: When removing hardware and the screws used to fasten it, be sure to place everything in a tin can or paper bag for safekeeping.

If you can't easily remove hardware, or if it just seems like too much bother, you can use masking tape or plastic wrap secured with rubber bands to protect what you don't want painted.

Remove switch plates and outlet plates for the same reasons that we suggested hardware be removed from doors. If you're going to paint the ceiling, unscrew ceiling fixtures and allow them to hang. Protect them with plastic wrap or plastic cleaners' bags. If you should encounter bare wires, turn off the electricity at its source and tape the wires. If the thought of fooling around with electrical wiring is just too scarifying, leave the ceiling fixtures in place and mask them, or paint around them very carefully.

Obviously, remove from the walls all pictures, mirrors, and other decorative objects, as well as shelves and their contents. If you plan to put these things back where they were, leave fasteners (nails, picture hooks, etc.) in place and paint over them. If you have a wall arrangement of pictures, mirrors, sconces, hangings, whatever, that you want to revise, do it now, before patching and painting. Put in new picture hooks and remove old ones that will no longer be needed. The time to change your mind and make a hole in the wall that turns out to be a mistake is now, when it can easily be corrected and patched, not later when you'd perhaps make a mistake on your nice new paint job. The new fasteners will be painted over. (Patching techniques are given in the following section.)

4. *Drop cloths vs. newspaper.* The final step of this stage is to throw something over furniture and floors to protect them. For furniture, drop cloths—enough to cover everything that has to be covered—are best. That's because a drop cloth drapes to conform to and completely cover the contours of whatever is underneath. Sheets of newspaper don't drape, they just sit flat.

Unless you tape them together and weight them down, any little draft could send them flying. Drop cloths cost money, but not much. They're worth the investment, especially if you're going to do a lot of painting.

5. *How to deal with spills, smudges, etc.* It's a good idea to keep an extra pile of newspapers handy so that if you spill a little paint on the floor, you can put a layer of paper over the spill. The idea is to prevent the possibility of someone's stepping into the spill and then tracking paint unawares to other parts of the house.

You might even want to buy a bag of sawdust and keep it nearby as you paint. Sawdust is just about the best thing going for sopping up paint, should you just happen to kick over a bucket. Don't open the bag unless you need the sawdust, though. Probably you *won't* need it.

It's best to deal with fresh paint smudges on windows by cleaning them off as you go. Use a cloth moistened with water if you're working with latex paint, a cloth moistened with mineral spirits if you're using alkyd paint.

No matter how carefully you've placed drop cloths or newspaper, when the job is done you may find a few dried-on paint spills. Often, these can be scraped away with a single-edge razor blade. Sometimes removal is easier if you apply linseed oil to the paint, then rub it away with a cloth dipped in more linseed oil. A really stubborn spot may need to be scrubbed off with fine steel wool. Just be careful not to take any of the surface material off with the paint.

PREPARING TO PAINT

An executive at a major paint company finally said outright what we'd been suspecting ever since we started researching this book: "A good paint job is 90 percent preparation."

If you thought painting was just throwing down drop cloths and going to work, the idea may come as a bit of a shock. Don't panic. He didn't mean that you'd have to put in ninety minutes of preparation for every ten minutes of painting you do. He did mean that a large part of the success of a paint job depends on factors that have nothing to do with how expertly you wield a roller or brush: factors such as whether the surface to be painted is clean or dirty, intact or chipped, peeling, cracking, full of holes, "virgin," or already painted—and with what.

Don't even so much as take the lid off a paint can until you're reasonably sure that ceilings and walls are in good enough condition to accept the paint properly. Hopefully, they *are* in good condition and you won't need to take more than one or two of the following measures. But just in case. . . .

DEGREASE AND DEDUST

Surfaces to be painted should be free of grease and dust, because paint just doesn't adhere very well to either.

Unless you're a housekeeping fanatic, you can be pretty sure that your kitchen ceiling and walls will need to be degreased. Wipe them down with a solution of powdered cleaner, such as Spic & Span, and water. (While you're at it, don't forget to wash woodwork and trim.) Rinse the surfaces thoroughly and allow them to dry before painting.

A professional painter tells us that he prefers ceilings and walls to be washed with a solution of trisodium phosphate (TSP for short) and water. He buys his in a paint-supply store, but TSP is also an ingredient in dishwasher detergent and you could use it in that form instead. A handful or so stirred into a bucket half filled with warm water should do it.

If your kitchen is painted with glossy or semigloss paint or enamel, you might want to degloss as you degrease. (Paint won't stick to a smooth, shiny surface any better than it does to grease.) See page 78 for how to degloss with TSP.

If there are very greasy areas that even TSP fails to cut through, you might want to try wiping them with a cloth or sponge moistened with benzine or paint thinner. But remember, both of these solvents are highly flammable. If your stove has a pilot light, it *must*—repeat, must—be extinguished before you use the stuff. Don't relight before the walls have been wiped thoroughly dry and the solvent has been removed from the area.

Ceilings and walls in other rooms may not need to be washed down. But they should be vacuumed free of loose dirt, dust, and cobwebs. Remember that windowsills, baseboards, and the tops of window- and doorframes are all big dust collectors. Seriously greased-up areas around switch plates, doorknobs, etc., should be wiped off with household cleaner or TSP and water. (We should add here that one marvelous professional painter, who probably does the best work in the whole state of New Jersey, washes *every* wall before painting. He feels you can't get best results without washing first.)

WHAT TO DO ABOUT STAINS

Water stains, the kind that remain after a leak has been fixed (and *please* don't paint over any water-damaged area until the source of the leak has been fixed), often have a way of bleeding through a fresh coat of paint and ruining it. So do some smoke stains and major grease stains, sap stains, and many other stains of known or possibly unknown origin.

You may be able to block a stain from bleeding through fresh paint by applying a coat of pigmented shellac sealer. See page 79 for how to apply the sealer. (Incidentally, in one store, when we asked for pigmented shellac sealer, the salesman hadn't the faintest notion what we were after; when we called it "stain-killer" he located it immediately.)

WHAT TO DO ABOUT FAULTY OLD PAINT

Old paint that is flaking, scaling, peeling, or chipping should be removed before you apply fresh paint. The reason is obvious, of course: New paint will simply coat the faulty old paint—and flake, scale, peel, or chip off along with it.

A paint scraper or putty knife with a wide blade is the best tool for removing big chips and flakes. A wire brush will take care of any small loose particles that are left behind by the scraper. When faulty old paint has been removed, use sandpaper to smooth the area so that it blends in with adjacent areas. Brush away sanding dust.

If the scraping and sanding exposes a layer of old paint of an entirely different color, apply one or two coats of the primer you'll be using on the rest of the wall. (If you're not using a primer, then apply one or two coats of the finish paint.) Allow each coat to dry before applying the next.

HOW TO MEND SMALL HOLES
AND FINE CRACKS

Nail holes and fine cracks can be patched very easily with spackling compound. Ask for the kind that comes in paste form and is made with a vinyl base. You'll also need a flexible putty knife.

To start, blow out or brush away any loose crumbs of plaster in the hole or crack. If the damaged area is much wider than, say, ¼ inch, take a sharp knife, ice pick, or similar tool and cut under the edges of the crack just slightly so that they are wider behind the opening than in front. This is called "undercutting." Undercutting gives the spackling compound something to hang on to.

Once again blow away any loose plaster crumbs. Then, with the putty knife, smear spackling compound into the opening. Force it in tightly by using firm "buttering" strokes back and forth across the opening. Finish by drawing the putty knife firmly along the edge of the opening. When the spackling compound is dry, smooth the area with sandpaper.

HOW TO DEGLOSS A SHINY SURFACE

Ceilings and walls finished with glossy (shiny) paint lack "tooth." They may be so hard and smooth that a fresh coat of paint will not stick—in which case, sooner or later, that new paint will begin to chip or peel. For this reason, any surface finished with glossy paint needs to be roughened up, or deglossed, before repainting.

- Sanding is one way to roughen up a shiny surface. Use medium-grit paper, wrap it around a block of wood so that it will be easier to hold on to, then rub it vigorously over the surfaces needing deglossing. This method obviously calls for a lot of elbow grease.

- Another method is to apply a liquid deglosser. These products are available in most well-stocked hardware and paint stores. They are highly flammable. Read the instructions printed on the label before using a deglosser, and be sure to heed all safety precautions.

- A third way to degloss—and degrease at the same time— is to mix up what is called a "saturated solution" of trisodium phosphate (TSP). To make it, fill a bucket halfway to the top with hot water. Pour in some TSP and stir to dissolve. Add more TSP and stir. Continue adding TSP until no more of it will dissolve in the water. At that point, you have a saturated solution.

  Be very careful in using it. The stuff is caustic. Wear gloves, long sleeves, and goggles just in case the solution should splash. If any of it should come into contact with your skin, rinse it off right away.

  To apply the solution, wipe it on with a sponge or cloth. Then rinse with clear water and wipe dry.

78

SECOND THOUGHTS ABOUT PRIMERS

Now you're ready to apply a coat of something. That something will be a primer, if you're using one. Otherwise, it will be the finish paint.

You may already have decided that you don't need a primer. But before you go ahead and open that can of finish paint, read the label to see what it says about primers. If the manufacturer of the paint strongly urges that a primer or undercoater of some kind be applied before the paint, you probably *should* go along with it.

Are you painting new wallboard that has never been painted before? Then you definitely should lay down a first coat of latex primer before applying the finish paint.

Are you using glossy or semigloss finish paint in the bathroom or kitchen? You'll get better-looking, longer-lasting results if you start out by applying an enamel undercoater.

Have you done a lot of patching preparatory to painting? By all means prime. Check the label of the paint can to see what primers are recommended as compatible with the paint. Or, apply a coat of pigmented shellac sealer. (This comes in white only, but you can tint it with universal tinting color, available at all paint stores, so that it will more closely approximate the color of the finish paint.)

Are you putting light finish paint over old dark paint? Once again you need a primer. Check the label to see which kind is most compatible with the finish paint.

Do you want a truly superb paint job—one that will last and last and last, one that you won't have to redo for years (unless you want to, because you're tired of the color)? You won't get that kind of paint job without a primer.

If you do decide to use a primer, or undercoater, apply it according to the step-by-step guides for painting ceilings and walls that follow.

STEP-BY-STEP GUIDE TO PAINTING
A CEILING

1. *The first step in painting a ceiling*: Paint neatly and cleanly along the ceiling's edges where it meets the walls—precision work that can't be done from the floor, not even with a roller or paint pad on an extension pole. You'll need to set up a good, sturdy stepladder. Or, you might want to improvise a scaffold.

A scaffold is more convenient because you can walk along it for a short distance. Thus, you won't have to move it as often as you would a ladder. To improvise a scaffold, you'll need a heavy plank, strong enough to take your weight and wide enough so that you don't have to do a balancing act while you're up on it. You'll also need two supports of equal height—two ladders, for example, or two sawhorses, or two sturdy chairs. Position the plank so that each end rests securely on a support. Obviously, if the supports are not of equal height, the plank will not be perfectly horizontal. That's not good. If you have any doubts about the sturdiness of the plank, or if you can't rig up two supports of equal height, better give up the idea of a scaffold and for safety's sake use a ladder instead.

A few words about ladder safety are in order here: Make sure the ladder is fully open, its two pairs of legs as far apart as possible and the metal arms straight. Never climb above the third step from the top. (If that doesn't bring you close enough to the ceiling to paint it easily, you need a taller ladder.) There should be a good couple of inches—more would be better—between the top of your head and the ceiling.

When you're up on a ladder, don't try to paint farther than you can easily reach without bending or stretching. Move the ladder instead. When you do move that ladder, get down off it to do so. Hard to believe, but we're told that some otherwise sensible people have used body English to try to "wiggle" a ladder over by a few feet—and ended up on the floor in a puddle of paint.

Now that you're up there on that ladder, take a trim brush, trim roller, or paint pad and cut along the edges of the ceiling. In layman's terms, this means to paint a "stripe" approximately two inches wide along the ceiling where it meets the wall. Cut along the edges of any ceiling fixtures, too. Cutting along the edges and fixtures as a first step allows you to get the precision painting over with all at once. Then you can speed ahead with the rest of the job.

Work carefully. The object is to paint as neat and clean an edge as you can, with little or no spillover onto the wall below. (Of course, if walls are to be painted the same color as the ceiling, neatness counts for less. Still, it's always a good idea to paint carefully rather than to slop it on.)

Paint as far around the edges of the ceiling as you can. But if you have moved the furniture into one corner, don't try to paint along that area. Save it for later.

2. *Switch to a wall brush* or wide roller or paint pad and set up the ladder or scaffold in a corner of the room. (Of course, you won't need ladder or scaffold if you're going to be working with an extension pole.) Face a source of light as you work; that way, you'll be able to see whether the paint is going on smoothly and evenly, with no skips.

3. *Work section by section* across the narrow dimension of the ceiling. In other words, if the ceiling is 9 feet by 12 feet, work in sections across the 9-foot width rather than along the 12-foot length.

4. *Starting with the corner*, paint the ceiling in approximately 3-foot by 3-foot sections.

Remember, if you are using a roller or pad, to start with a zigzag M shape, with the first stroke going *away* from you. If you are using a brush, begin by laying on a few dabs of paint. Fill in the section, then smooth and feather the edges. (For a refresher course in roller, brush, and pad-painting techniques, turn back to the appropriate section of Chapter III.)

5. *When you've painted in sections* from one wall all the way across the short length of the ceiling to the opposite wall, move the ladder or scaffold back about three feet, then work across the ceiling again in the opposite direction, being careful to feather the edges of new paint into the feathered edges of the previously painted sections.

6. *When you've painted as far as you can go* without bumping into the furniture in that far corner, stop. Move the furniture to the center of the room. "Cut" along the remaining edges of the ceiling. Then continue painting the remainder of the ceiling in sections, as before.

STEP-BY-STEP GUIDE FOR PAINTING WALLS

The proper sequence for painting a room, remember, is to do the ceiling first, then trim (window and door frames, baseboards, etc.); then masonry, if any, and finally, walls. For how to paint trim, see Chapter VI. Chapter VII tells how to paint masonry. When those surfaces are finished, go to work on the walls.

1. *Start in a corner*—a right-hand corner, if you are right-handed, a left-hand corner, if you are left-handed. Paint one entire wall at a time. With a trim brush, narrow roller, or small paint pad, paint a neat, clean two-inch-wide strip along the entire wall where it meets the ceiling. Then, cut down the corners, where wall meets wall. Finally, cut along the bottom of the wall where it meets baseboard or floor. Finally, cut a two-inch strip around door and window frames as well as any built-in cabinets, masonry, switch plates, etc., on the wall.

2. *Switch to a wide tool*—roller, wall brush, or paint pad. Beginning in the corner, near the ceiling, paint the wall in approximately 3-foot by 3-foot sections.

If you are using a roller or a paint pad, start with a zigzag M shape, with the first stroke going in an upward direction. If you're using a brush, start by laying on a few slaps of paint. Fill in the sections. Feather the edges, then smooth the paint with long, light, even strokes. (For more about roller-, brush-, and pad-painting techniques, see Chapter III.)

3. *Start the second section*: Do this below the first, the third below the second, and so on until you reach the bottom of the wall. Don't forget to feather the edges of each new section into the feathered edges of the previously painted section above it, then go over the area where they meet, with long, light strokes.

4. *Back to the top of the wall*: This is where you start the next new section. Continue to paint the wall in sections, working top to bottom, until the wall is finished.

V

The Problem Wall

When you're painting over problem walls—badly gouged, bulging, cracked, stained, mildewed, or otherwise damaged surfaces—special preparation is necessary, of course. Now all this special preparation takes time and work (a good deal of time and work in some cases), but in the end it's worth every bit of the energy expended. In other words, it's entirely possible to turn most problem walls into good-as-new walls.

And speaking of new walls—those, too, sometimes require special preparation, even though they aren't exactly problem walls. Since most, if not all, of today's new walls are made of wallboard (also known as Sheetrock, gypsum board, dry wall, etc.), we'll begin with the preparation of new, never-painted wallboard.

NEW, NEVER-PAINTED WALLBOARD

Generally, new wallboard needs only priming before it is painted. But if there are any defects in the surface—if the seams are joined together in a messy fashion or nails are popping or protruding from the surface—corrections must be made before you paint. If not, the defects will become even more glaringly apparent when the paint is applied.

1. *The seams or joints.* The seams between the panels of wallboard must be properly covered with joint cement and tape so they will not be noticeable when painted. If this work has been done sloppily, you can remedy it by applying one or two additional coats of joint cement (available in paint and hardware stores) with a wide putty knife, feathering out the edges so the cement blends smoothly with the wallboard surface on each side. Let the first coat of cement dry completely before applying the second. Sand the joint smooth when your patching has dried, using fine-grit sandpaper.

If the seams haven't been covered with tape and cement (outrageous if they haven't), do the job yourself before you paint. Joint tape (which is usually a perforated paper tape) and cement come packaged together and are not difficult to apply. Just mix the cement according to the directions on the package and apply it over the seam with a wide putty knife. While it's still wet, press a length of the tape over the seam and work it into the cement until it's almost covered. Let this dry hard, then apply more cement over the seam to completely cover the tape. Be sure to feather out the edges with your putty knife so the cement blends smoothly with the wallboard on either side of the seam. When this second layer of cement is completely dry, apply one more layer of cement—using an extra-wide putty knife or a plasterer's trowel—to fill in any rough spots and continue feathering the edges so the seam will be invisible when it is painted. Sand the seam smooth, with medium-grit and then fine sandpaper, when it is dry.

2. *Nail protrusions.* Nail heads should dent or "dimple" the wallboard, but not break the surface. Before painting, you should conceal the nails by covering them with joint cement or spackle, feathered so that it blends with the wallboard, and sanded smooth

when dry. If the nail happens to protrude above the surface, you can buy a special knife with a "hammer handle" (available in hardware stores) to sink the nail properly into the wallboard.

3. *Priming and painting.* When the seams and nail dimples are covered so they'll be invisible when painted, vacuum the surface thoroughly to get rid of any dust and loose matter. Then prime the entire wall with a latex emulsion primer. (Latex primers seem to work better than alkyd primers on unpainted wallboard because they don't disturb the fibers of the thick paper surface.)

NOTE: Don't skip the primer and use a first coat of your top-coat paint for the job. The primer is specially formulated to prevent undue penetration of the paint into the paper surface of the wallboard. If you worry that you'll have trouble covering the primer (which is white) with your top coat, you can tint it toward the color of the top coat by adding to it (or asking your paint dealer to add) a little universal color. Universal color, a pigment formulation used only for tinting, comes in a tube or a can and is available in paint stores. It can be used to tint paint of just about any formulation. You could also mix in a little of your top-coat paint to tint the primer.

When the primer is dry, paint the wallboard with any latex paint. Or, if you're working in the kitchen or bathroom, use a washable, durable, gloss or semigloss latex paint.

VERY OLD, MANY-TIMES-PAINTED WALLS

In old houses or apartments, you're likely to find walls that have been covered with many, many, *many* layers of paint. And there's no way of telling what kind of paint was used on the wall thirty or forty or more years back. This is especially true in old apartment houses where the walls were repainted every year or two or three, according to the requirements of a lease. Uncannily—and unfortunately—a coat of paint that was applied to the wall many years ago, and successfully covered by layer upon layer of paint, may suddenly act up and give you trouble.

The most effective, though not the easiest, way to handle the problem is to remove all the old paint on the wall. But this is probably more work than you're interested in, especially if you're renting the apartment and don't intend to stay for long. In which case, go ahead and paint.

But be sure to use an alkyd paint on the wall. Somewhere among those several dozen layers of paint, sizing made with water-soluble animal glue was probably applied to the wall. Water-base latex paint will act as a remover, peeling off the new coat of paint along with the old.

To do the best possible job on the wall, wash down the surface with detergent and water, rinse off the detergent, and, when the wall is dry, sand it (even if it isn't glossy). Apply an alkyd primer-sealer and then paint with the best-quality alkyd paint you can find.

Removing the old paint. If, however, you decide to remove the old paint from the wall, by all means don't use a blowtorch to do the job! It's too dangerous. For all you know, one of those many coats of old paint may be highly flammable.

Instead, use a commercial paint remover (available in paint and hardware stores) or an electric belt sander (which you can rent from a hardware dealer or a tool-rental agency).

If you use commercial paint remover, buy the semipaste, non-flammable kind that doesn't require a wipe-away with paint thinner. It also won't run off the wall before it has had a chance to work, as liquid paint removers do.

But be prepared for a messy job. Dress for the occasion in old clothes and wear rubber or plastic gloves and eye protection. Also cover any exposed skin with Vaseline petroleum jelly or cold cream—and work with the windows wide open for adequate ventilation. You don't want to asphyxiate yourself while you're beautifying your home.

With an old paintbrush, apply the paint remover in a thick layer with a minimum of back-and-forth stroking. Once it's on the wall, don't touch it until it's time to scrape it off. After letting the remover soak into the surface (for as long as the label of the product you're using specifies), scrape it off with a dull putty knife. Or use coarse steel wool and a stiff brush dipped repeatedly in water. If all the paint doesn't scrape or scrub off with one application of the paint remover, repeat the procedure. Or, if you see after the first few scrapes that the first coat of remover isn't doing the job, apply a second equally heavy coat of remover right over the first, wait the specified time, and then scrape. You may still have to repeat the process two or three times to do a thorough job. Then, when the wall is completely dry, sand it with fine sandpaper.

An electric belt sander is by far the quickest and easiest—and wisest—tool to use for removing the paint. But be prepared for some heavy work. Literally. The machine itself seems to weigh a ton (not literally). And be sure to close all doors to the room you're working in, or you'll have fine grit all over the house. But keep the windows wide open—and wear adequate eye protection (goggles or glasses). Just in case there's leaded paint on the wall—and there probably is—you should also wear a painter's nose-and-mouth mask. It's not a good idea to breathe in any of the sanding dust from leaded paints.

Whatever method you use for removing the paint, be sure to apply a primer-sealer before applying the top coat.

THE PAPERED WALL

Yes, you *can* paint over wallpaper, if the wallpaper is not peeling off the wall. Painting over wallpaper is not the best thing to do, for a number of reasons, but people do it all the time. I've even done it myself. Once.

If the wallpaper is peeling from the wall, you can lift the paper a little and repaste it with ready-to-use wallpaper paste you can buy wherever wallpaper is sold, following the directions on the container. Once the peeling wallpaper is repaired, give the paste adequate time to dry before you paint. However, be aware that if the paper is poorly pasted, the weight of a coat of paint may pull it loose again. Also, the seams where the strips of wallpaper are joined will become unpleasantly visible once the wall is painted, especially if you're using a light-color paint. If you decide to remove the painted-over wallpaper at a later date, it will be more difficult to remove than if it had not been painted.

NOTE: Don't try painting over vinyl wall-coverings, which are very likely "strippable." That is, they can be removed easily by prying loose a corner and pulling them off the wall. Some of the newer wallpapers are strippable as well. Test an inconspicuous corner of the paper you want to paint over to see if it pries loose easily. Also avoid painting over flocked wallpaper unless you think you'll like the effect.

Avoiding pattern bleed-through. If the wallpaper you're painting over is brightly patterned, the pattern will most likely show through the new paint. This can be avoided, however, if you prime the paper with a pigmented shellac-base sealer such as B-I-N or Enamelac, which are widely known among professional painters as "stain-killers." These sealers yield a flat white finish that is dry to the touch within fifteen minutes and can be painted over in forty-five minutes. To tint them closer to the color of your top coat, mix in some universal color, which you can buy from your paint dealer. But never tint a shellac-base sealer with top-coat paint. Shellac-base sealers have an alcohol base, which is incompatible with the water base of latex paints or the oil base of alkyds.

Shellac-base sealers are thinned with denatured alcohol rather than turpentine or paint thinner (mineral spirits). Although the manufacturers advise against thinning them, they dry so quickly that some thinning may be necessary after the can has been open awhile. Denatured alcohol is also used to clean up after the job is done.

Shellac-base sealers are best applied with a brush, although a roller with a short nap also may be used.

Removing old wallpaper. You really will save a lot of future headaches by removing old wallpaper before painting. If the paper isn't strippable as described above, you can remove it in two ways: with a commercial wallpaper remover, which you can buy in a paint or hardware store; or with a steamer, which you may be able to rent from your paint-and-wallpaper dealer or through a tool-rental agency. (Steamers are not available for rental in many localities, however.) Whichever method you use, be prepared for a messy job!

Wallpaper remover is actually a "surface tension reducer" that you add to a bucket of water to make the water *wetter*—so wet, in fact, that it will soak through the paper and soften the paste underneath. One remover even has a special enzyme that eats into and softens the paste on the back of the old paper. Apply the remover to an entire vertical strip of wallpaper with a sponge or a brush and then peel off the paper with a putty knife. Gather each strip of paper as you peel it off the wall and dispose of it in a large trash bag. Otherwise it will stick to whatever it lands on! Be sure to protect your floor with newspapers and/or drop cloths. When there are several layers of paper on the wall, remove one layer at a time. (If you are living in a very old house, watch out; you could be uncovering and damaging very interesting old papers. Get in touch with the nearest historical society to find an expert to advise you.)

The steamer literally steams the paper to loosen it. But the paper still has to be peeled or scraped from the wall. The machine consists of a tank in which water is heated to create steam, which flows through a hose to a perforated plate you hold against the wall. Here are some tips for working with a steamer:

- Hold the plate to the wall in one spot for fifteen to twenty seconds, then move it slowly along as you scrape off the wallpaper with your other hand. Use a putty knife to do the scraping. Or work with a partner. This job is less clumsy if there are two of you working together.

- Work from the bottom up so that the rising steam can begin to soften the paper farther on up the wall as you're scraping and steaming away on the lower sections.

- By the same logic, if you're removing wallpaper from the ceilings as well as from the walls, do the walls first.

- So the room won't become overly filled with steam, close all the doors but open the windows.

- Regardless of how good your ventilation is, the steam will naturally collect near the ceiling and leave watermarks as it cools. So if you do use a steamer to remove the old wallpaper, count on painting the ceiling after the job is done.

- Protect your floors with drop cloths or newspapers. Water may drip off the ceiling as you work, and paper will probably drop to the floor as well, sticking to just about anything it lands on.

NOTE: If you're removing wallpaper from wallboard that wasn't painted or primed before the paper was applied, be prepared for trouble. It will be almost impossible to remove the paper without damaging the surface of the wallboard. So remove whatever paper comes off easily, then prime the surface with one or more coats of the best quality primer-sealer you can buy. When it's dry, apply your top coat.

Removing old wallpaper that has been painted over.   As we said, this is much more difficult than removing wallpaper that hasn't been painted. The coating of paint will in large measure prevent the steam or wallpaper remover from soaking through the paper to soften the paste. But it's not an insurmountable problem.

The easiest solution is to scratch up the painted wallpaper as thoroughly as you can with the coarsest grade of sandpaper you can find. It isn't necessary to *remove* the paint, just scratch it up enough so that the steam or water can penetrate it. Then remove the paper as described before. If there are stubborn spots, scratch them up again with sandpaper and repeat the removal process.

Getting rid of the paste residue.   After removing the wallpaper, by whatever method, scrub the wall with a strong detergent and hot (very hot) water to remove any paste that is left. If there is paste remaining, it will interfere with the smooth application of primer and paint and may prevent them from drying properly as well.

Even if there appears to be no paste remaining on the wall, it's still a good idea to wash the surface before going further. A solution of trisodium phosphate (available in hardware stores as TSP) and water works the quickest. Use one cup of TSP per gallon of hot water and scrub with a stiff brush. Rinse with warm water, and when the wall is dry, sand down any rough spots with medium-grit sandpaper. Then prime the wall, preferably with an alkyd-base primer-sealer—and, finally, paint.

THE GLUE-DAMAGED WALL

While wallpaper paste can be removed from a wall with TSP and hot water, the pastes and adhesives used to apply tile are not as easily removed. Most adhesives, however, will dissolve with either lacquer thinner, acetone, or paint remover. Since these are extremely volatile, flammable substances, be sure to take precautions when you use them—and keep the windows wide open!

You could, instead, use a belt sander and medium-grit sandpaper to do the job. If your hardware dealer doesn't know where a belt sander can be rented, look in the Yellow Pages for the name of a tool-rental agency.

After removing the glue, sand away any rough spots and then scrub the wall with TSP and hot water. Let dry and sand again if necessary. Then prime the wall with an alkyd-base primer-sealer before painting.

THE BADLY STAINED WALL

Stains from water and fire damage as well as stains from knotty, sappy wood (in panelling or wainscoting) will invariably bleed through ordinary paint. But you have a good chance of avoiding the bleed-through if you prime the stained wall with a pigmented shellac-base sealer, such as B-I-N or Enamelac, of the kind long used by professional painters as stain-killers. For the best results, prime the entire wall, not just the stains, and use two coats of the shellac-base primer if necessary.

As we said in the earlier section on painting over patterned wallpaper, shellac-base sealers yield a flat-white finish that can be tinted toward the color of the top coat with universal color, available from your paint dealer. This sealer dries quickly and a second coat can be applied forty-five minutes after the first one. The best method of application is with a brush, but a roller with a short nap may also be used. The cleanup is done with denatured alcohol, which is also used for any thinning that may be necessary. Just about any paint may be used for the top coat.

THE GOUGED, CRACKED, UNSIGHTLY WALL

Plaster walls. When repairing holes and cracks of a substantial size in plaster walls, you'll need to mix up a batch of patching plaster. (Don't mix it up until you're *ready*. It sets very quickly.) You'll also need a large putty knife.

First remove any loose plaster from the area and take a look to see what's inside the opening. It could be that there is just more plaster back there. Or, perhaps the opening exposes vertical strips of wood or metal—"lath" is what those strips are called. Either way, mix up some patching plaster according to the directions on the bag. With a sponge or cloth dipped in water, moisten all surfaces of the opening, including the lath if it is exposed.

Scoop up some plaster with the putty knife and press it firmly all around under the edges of the opening. Scoop up some more and force it up tight against the lath or plaster at the center and back of the opening. Pack it in, but don't try to fill a deep opening all at once. It's better to apply two or more layers of patching plaster, one over the other.

When the first layer is in place and still moist, draw a few wavy lines across it with a sharp tool. This is called "scoring." Scoring will provide better adhesion for the next layer of plaster.

Wait until the fresh plaster is hard and dry. Then moisten it and, again working from the edges toward the center of the opening, pack in a new layer. The final layer should be level with the surface of the wall. With a putty knife, smooth it off as evenly as possible. When the plaster is completely dry, sand away any roughness and prime the patch with one or two coats of the primer you will be using on the rest of the wall.

If you peer inside an opening and it looks as though there's nothing back there on which to build up new layers of plaster, stuff crumpled pieces of newspaper into the hole. Keep stuffing until there's enough newspaper packed tightly into the hole to act as a base for new plaster. Next, mix up some plaster. Moisten the exposed surfaces of the opening. Then, with the putty knife, press plaster all around under the edges of the opening. Force more plaster up against the packed-in newspaper. Score the fresh plaster. Allow it to dry. Then apply another layer, working from the edges toward the center. The final layer should be even with the surface of the wall. Smooth it with the putty knife. When it is completely dry, sand away any roughness, and prime the patch with one or two coats of the primer you will be using on the rest of the wall.

Wallboard. If the hole in your wall is a big one and the surface is wallboard (Sheetrock, gypsum board, etc.), you can try repairing it with a "plug" cut from a piece of gypsum board. For this job, you'll need a sharp knife or small saw, a putty knife, contact cement, spackling compound and, of course, the piece of wallboard—a leftover scrap will do fine if you have one.

With a knife or a saw, cut two pieces from the new or scrap wallboard. The first piece should be rectangular in shape and somewhat longer and wider than the hole in the wall. This rectangular section is the "plug." Then cut a strip that is narrower and about 2 inches longer than the plug. This strip is the backing.

94

Use the plug as a pattern. Place it up against the wall over the hole and trace around it lightly with a pencil. Then, with the knife or saw, cut through the wall along the penciled line. Remove loose pieces. There should now be an opening in the wall of about the same size as the plug. Check to see if the plug fits into the opening. If it doesn't, trim the plug to fit.

Now apply contact cement liberally to each end of the backing strip. Insert the strip through the opening in the wall and pull it up against the back of the wall so that it bridges the opening. Hold it there for a few moments—long enough so that the cement has a chance to grab. Allow several hours for the cement to dry.

When the cement on the backing is completely dry, apply a liberal amount of cement to the plug. Insert the plug into the opening and press it gently up against the backing strip. Hold it long enough for the cement to grab again.

Allow several hours for the cement on the plug to dry. Then use a putty knife to force spackling compound into the seams between plug and wall. Spackle over the plug itself, too. When the spackling compound is dry, sand it smooth. (You may find that you need to apply more spackling compound to further close up the seams.) When the seams are filled, dry, and level with the surface, prime the patch with one or two coats of the primer you'll use to finish the wall.

Instead of making the patch yourself, you may be able to find a wallboard-patching kit in a hardware store. Follow the instructions that come with the kit.

THE MILDEWED WALL

Mildew is a splotchy-looking fungus—it looks like gray dirt —that attaches itself to a painted wall, especially when there's a bit of moisture in the room. It's commonly found in basements and bathrooms, but no room is immune to it.

Mildew must be removed before you repaint or, in the process of painting, you'll spread it to other areas and be left, in due time, with gray, dirty-looking mildew spores over the entire wall. And, if you paint over a mildewed surface, the mildew will come right through the new coat of paint.

To kill mildew, scrub the affected area with a solution made up of ⅔ cup TSP (trisodium phosphate), ⅓ cup strong powdered laundry detergent, 1 quart chlorine bleach (such as Clorox), plus enough hot water to fill up a gallon bucket or jug. Scrub the area vigorously with the solution and a stiff scrub brush, then rinse it thoroughly with warm water. While you work, wear rubber gloves and goggles or glasses and keep the windows and doors wide open. If you begin to feel dizzy or start to gasp, take a *long* break. And *don't* try to mix up a stronger solution by adding a little ammonia to it. Ammonia plus chlorine bleach make a dangerous, vaporous concoction that can do damage to your respiratory system and, at worst, may be fatal.

When you know that mildew is going to be a problem on a painted surface (if you've just removed it from a wall, you can expect that it will return), either use a paint that contains a mildewcide, or make the paint you're using mildew-resistant by adding a special fungicide you can buy at the paint store. Mildew spores are tricky, however. Sometimes they thrive no matter what you do. In such cases the best you can do is to keep them from spreading.

THE PAINT-FAILED WALL

Peeling, checkered, alligatored, wrinkled, sagging, and never-quite-dry paint—all these conditions are called "failed" paint.

The cause of paint failure is frequently inadequate preparation of the surface before painting. But sometimes it results from the use of low-quality paint or from moisture damage caused by leaky pipes or a structural defect. Here is how to recognize the conditions and remedy them.

1. *Peeling paint.* This is often the result of a serious moisture problem somewhere behind the wall—perhaps a leaky pipe

or, as happened to one of my neighbors, the mortar holding together the exterior brick is in bad shape and moisture is seeping through. In this case, most of the paint on the wall will be peeling and the surface will feel damp and cold to the touch. Whatever the cause, the moisture problem must be remedied before there is any sense in repainting the wall.

Peeling paint, however, also occurs when the wall was not properly prepared for the paint—when, for example, the paint was applied over a dirty, greasy surface, or over a glossy surface that was not sanded to degloss it before painting.

To remedy: The peeling paint must be scraped off the wall with a wire brush and the area sanded to feather any rough edges. Then the wall should be cleaned with strong detergent and water and, if the surface is glossy, it should be deglossed with sandpaper when it is dry. A primer should then be applied, followed by a top coat or two.

2. *Checkered and alligatored paint.* When paint checks, a network of tiny cracks shows up on the surface of the top coat. Alligatoring is an exaggeration of this condition, with the surface so rough it resembles alligator skin. Frequently the problem occurs when the surface has not been properly prepared (cleaned, sanded, primed), or when poor-quality paint is used as a top coat and there is not enough binder in it to adhere to the paint beneath. Checkering also occurs when a second coat of paint is applied before the first coat is completely dry.

To remedy: The only solution is to remove the damaged paint, and then to prepare properly the surface before repainting.

3. *Chalking paint.* Paint may become "chalky" if only one coat is applied over a porous surface that wasn't sealed or primed. If the paint has good hiding power, the one coat will, at first, seem adequate. But the binder in the paint will be quickly absorbed by the porous surface, leaving only a thin coat of pigment which appears chalky and powdered.

Some flat latex wall-paints in dark colors—especially dark blues, grays, and blacks, even those of the best quality—have a tendency to chalk when something rubs against them.

The remedy: Apply another coat or two of paint. Or apply a primer and then a top coat of paint.

4. *Wavy, sagging paint.* A wavy, irregular, sagging surface is sometimes due to inexperienced brushmanship—that is, the painter failed to brush out the paint consistently and evenly so that, unfortunately, it is thick in some places, thin in others, and who-knows-what in between.

To remedy: Let the paint dry thoroughly and then sand the wall smooth and add another coat of paint—this time applied with a roller or paint pad.

5. *Wrinkling.* Wrinkled paint is paint that has dried with a rough, wrinkled texture. This happens when the paint is applied too thickly, so that the top surface dries while the underside of it remains soft. Wrinkling also sometimes occurs when paint is applied to a cold surface on a hot, dry day.

To remedy: The wrinkled paint must be removed from the wall before repainting.

6. *A tacky, never-quite-dry surface.* When a painted wall never quite dries, it's a pretty good sign that the paint used was not of good quality. It also means that the weather was probably quite humid when the job was done and/or the paint was applied too thickly. A good paint will dry despite either of these conditions.

To remedy: Remove the paint and do the job over.

TEXTURED PAINT: THE INSTANT PROBLEM-SOLVER

After reading most of the above, you may feel discouraged. It's so much work fixing and priming patches and stains. It's so much work repairing poorly jointed wallboard—as it also is fixing lumps and bumps and depressions in a wall.

Textured paint to the rescue: One coat will cover almost any surface, so that you will never know what irregularities lurk beneath. (I would still remove a tacky, never-quite-dry paint from the wall, however.) '

Better yet, textured paint is in vogue. It's popular decoratively and will probably remain popular for a number of years to come.

Some textured paints are ready-mixed latexes in a thick liquid of a semipaste consistency. Others come packaged as powders that must be mixed with water before using. (We prefer the ready-mixed variety.)

1. *To apply*: Most textured paints are easily applied with a roller or a brush. First a thick coat of the paint goes on a section of the wall, and then the paint must be textured or "worked" immediately afterward with a texturing tool. You can use almost anything as your texturing tool—a sponge, a comb, a paintbrush, a roller, a whisk broom, or a plasterer's trowel. The job is best done as a two-person operation, with one of you applying the paint and the other texturing it; this is the preferred way for amateur painters to do the job.

Sand paint or sand-finish paint, however, goes on in one operation and needn't be textured after the application. Sand paint has tiny granules added to it (though sometimes they are pre-mixed in the paint) to produce a gritty sand finish. It applies best with a roller that has a short nap. It is particularly effective on ceilings.

2. *Texturing or "working" the paint.* One easy way to work the finish is to apply a heavy coat of the paint with a brush and then go over it with an ordinary roller. If the roller has a short nap, you'll achieve a mild stipple effect. But if the roller has a long nap, the stipple will be coarser and heavier.

It is equally easy to use a sponge to achieve an allover, mildly stippled pattern. Just dab the sponge on the surface of the wet paint.

A classical stucco-like effect results from using an ordinary plasterer's trowel on the wet paint—patting, pressing, and swirling it for the desired texture.

You can also simulate stucco by holding a wide paintbrush

so it is almost flat with the wall but not yet touching it. Then flick it lightly into the paint and repeat the motion to cover the paint with an allover pattern. Or use a whisk broom or a stiff brush to create swirls. Or see what happens when you comb through the wet paint with an ordinary (but fairly sturdy) comb or a notched trowel. Try combing through the paint in short strokes made at different angles.

Whatever you do, don't be overly concerned with the regularity of the pattern. Part of the charm of textured paint is in its irregularity.

3. *Disadvantages of textured paint.* If you do use textured paint, don't expect to get the same coverage you would with an ordinary paint (which is approximately 400 square feet per gallon). Because textured paint is so heavily applied, a gallon covers only about 90 square feet, give or take a few square feet. If you're painting a large room, plan for an expensive project.

Also, most textured paint is made only in white, but it can be tinted to a pastel color with a tube or can of universal color, which is available in most paint stores; many paint dealers will be happy to do the tinting for you. Or, you can apply the textured paint and, when it is dry, paint over it with any color of paint you want, using a brush or a roller with a long nap to get into the crevices.

Finally, if you've had textured paint on the wall for a while and decide that you don't like it, it's very difficult to remove— not impossible, but difficult. If you try removing it with paint remover, it might turn into a lifetime job. Better to rent a belt sander—or buy one if there's no rental agency available—and power-sand the paint away. This is a messy job. Close all doors to the room you're working in, or the grit will fly all over the house—but open all the windows. Wear old clothes and eye protection—and before you begin, cover with drop cloths both the floor and any furnishings too heavy to move out of the room. Good luck! (Of course, you could always put up new wallboard instead . . .)

VI

How to Paint Doors, Windows & Other Trim

First of all, what *is* trim?

To the professional painter, "trim" means baseboards, wainscoting, doors, and doorframes as well as window frames, windowsills, and sashwork. Long ago, these things were always made of wood. Most still are. Here, we're including with this group shutters and built-in cabinets and cupboards—also usually but not always made of wood.

Trim is somewhat more difficult to paint than large flat surfaces such as ceilings and walls—more difficult, that is, unless you know professional painters' tricks for making short work of them. That's what this chapter is about.

WHY IT'S BEST TO PAINT TRIM
BEFORE WALLS

You already know that when you're painting an entire room it's best to paint the ceiling first. Then trim. Then walls. Back in Chapter IV there was a brief explanation of why this sequence works best. Here's a more precise rationale.

Because of the many grooved surfaces and narrow edges involved, painting trim is tricky. No matter how careful you are, chances are you'll get some trim paint on adjacent walls. You're far more likely to get trim paint on walls than to get wall paint on trim. If the walls have already been painted and you get trim paint on them, you have to go back and touch up the wall paint. The problem is, such touch-ups aren't always successful; you can usually tell where the finish has been tampered with. Better to do trim first, then cover up any mistakes you make on the walls later with the wall paint.

HOW TO CHOOSE THE RIGHT PAINT
FOR TRIM

Traditionally, high-gloss or semigloss paint or enamel has been the first choice for trim. There's more than mere convention behind this preference for shiny trim surfaces. Of all surfaces in the house, trim probably gets the roughest treatment. Baseboards take a beating from, among other things, furniture legs, the vacuum cleaner, and, if there are small children about, from tricycles and toy trucks. In time, doors and doorframes acquire an assortment of greasy and nongreasy smudges. Windowsills collect dust and grit. And so on. Because they dirty up so fast, these surfaces get more than their fair share of scrubbing. Thus, they need the most durable, scrubbable paint. And the shinier the paint, the smoother and more durable it is.

Many people dislike the glare of high-gloss paint. If you're one of them, then by all means choose a semigloss instead. Semigloss is the current most popular choice for trim.

As we pointed out in the chapter about paint, semigloss paint and enamel are available in either alkyd or latex formulations. Which is best? Alkyds still rate higher in terms of durability and scrubbability. This is not to say that latex semigloss is *not* durable and scrubbable—only that it is somewhat less so than an alkyd semigloss. As a nonprofessional painter, alkyd's greater durability may be less important to you in the short run than the easier application and cleanup of latex. In other words, take your choice.

As for color, think twice about trying to match semigloss trim paint to the color of the flat or satin-finish paint that you plan to use on walls. Manufacturers aim for color consistency in their products, but they do not always get it because of slight color variations that can occur from batch to batch of paint, variations that are beyond the manufacturers' control. So, while a perfect match is possible, don't count on it.

Since an attempt at matching two different kinds of paint could have rather jarring results, it's usually a better idea to think in terms of a trim color that harmonizes or contrasts with the walls.

On the other hand, if matching is more important to you than durability, there's no rule that says you *can't* use the same flat or satin-finish paint on trim that you use on the walls. One thing that works rather well if the color you have chosen is a subdued and subtle one custom-mixed by formula by your paint store (see page 38) is deliberately to paint the trim the same color but ever so slightly lighter or darker than the walls. Also, if one wall in the room receives much less light from your windows than the other, *it* could be painted a shade or two lighter and will end up looking the same as the others. It is often the *window* wall, if there is only one, that benefits most by this treatment.

HOW TO PREPARE TRIM
FOR PAINTING

Don't be discouraged by the sheer *number* of steps that follow. We've given suggestions for remedying almost every conceivable kind of trim problem. It's possible—even probable—that most of what follows won't apply to the trim in your house or apartment. In fact, you may need to do little more than vacuum away the dust before you paint. However, do at least read through the following section.

1. *Hardware*: As suggested in Chapter IV, if you can easily do so, remove knobs and other hardware from doors—windows, cupboards, and cabinets, too. Some painters also like to take doors off their hinges. (They say painting is easier that way.) If you do take the doors down, you probably shouldn't remove the hinges unless they show signs of "paint sickness." (See next step.)

Should you paint the hinges? Yes, of course, if they've been painted before. The answer is still yes if they're unpainted but made of metal other than solid brass. Hinges not made of brass tend to lose their shine in time and there's no really good way to polish them. They may even begin to corrode. A coat of paint will be more attractive in the long run.

2. *Paint sickness*: Inspect all trim surfaces for what the pros often call paint sickness. Paint-sick surfaces are those that have been buried under so many layers of globby old paint that the original contours have lost their definition. Windowsills and sash-work in some old houses and apartment buildings often are stricken with this condition. So are the edges of between-room doors and of cupboard and cabinet doors. Often, the old-paint buildup is so heavy, the doors balk and won't close properly any-more.

You can treat the condition with a chemical paint-remover. Get the nonflammable kind that comes in semipaste consistency, if you can. This is the easiest to work with because the material is less likely to run down and off vertical surfaces. Be sure to follow to the letter all instructions for safe usage printed on the label. Hinges and other hardware can be immersed in the chemical; then softened paint can be scrubbed away with a wire brush.

Another way to fight paint sickness is to attack it with a mechanical paint stripper. These devices are attached to and pow-ered by a quarter-inch drill. Many people have had good results with the mechanical stripper, but it's unsuitable for use on some surfaces. (A friend, for example, used his on marble. The paint came off quickly and easily, but the marble was scratched in the process.) Need we say it again? If you decide to invest in one of these contraptions, don't use it until you've read and thoroughly understood the instructions that come with it.

A third way to cope with paint sickness is to scrape it away with a paint scraper, sharp knife, or sharp single-edge razor blade (in a holder, of course; blade holders can be bought in any hardware store). Or, if you're dealing with quite a large paint-sick surface, you could use a plane. Just be careful not to plane away any of the wood beneath the problem paint.

NOTE: After curing paint sickness with a mechanical paint stripper or sharp tool, smooth the surface by going over it with medium-grit sandpaper.

3. *Are the window frames tight?* Check to see that there are no openings where window frames meet walls. If there are gaping spaces, clean away loose material, wipe the opening with mineral spirits, then seal with caulking compound. Tell the hardware-store salesman why you need the caulking compound, and make sure to buy the kind that can be painted over. Use the material according to the instructions that come with it. Allow adequate drying time before painting.

4. *Pull nails and remove hardware* that no longer serves any particular purpose. The trim in many middle-aged and older houses and apartment buildings is studded with an assortment of odd nails, window-shade brackets, etc., put up by previous occupants and never removed. Clean away any loose particles left in nail holes or screw holes. Spot-prime the openings with shellac or a primer recommended on the label of the finish paint. When the primer is dry, fill the openings with water putty—also known as wood putty. Mix up the water putty according to instructions on the container. The material dries quickly, so don't prepare a batch until just before you're going to use it. Lightly moisten the area to be filled, then press the putty into the hole with a knife or your finger. Sand it smooth when it is dry.

5. *Remove old paint that is chipping,* peeling, or flaking. Use a wire brush or paint scraper. Be careful not to gouge the

wood under the old paint. With sandpaper, smooth and blend in the areas so that there are no hard edges to show through the new paint.

6. *Use water putty to fill in* where surfaces are badly chipped or gouged, or to replace small sections that are missing altogether. Water putty is fun to work with. It adheres well and can be molded into just about any shape. With skillful use of it, old chewed-up woodwork can be made to look brand-new again, or almost. Spot-prime first. Use shellac or a primer recommended on the label of the finish paint. When the primer is dry, lightly moisten the area to be patched, then apply the putty. Use any handy tool to help you work the material to the desired shape. Or, mold it with your hands. Allow ample time for drying. Then sand smooth.

7. *Remove any waxy residue* from baseboards and the bottoms of doors and paneling. Paint won't stick to wax. (You can assume that there's a film of wax on surfaces that meet the floor in any room where floor wax is regularly used.) To remove wax, wipe with a cloth saturated in benzine or mineral spirits. Both are highly flammable; be guided accordingly. Scrub with fine soapless steel wool. Then wipe dry.

8. *Scrub seriously greased-up areas* with all-purpose household cleaner or a solution of TSP (trisodium phosphate) and water. Rinse and wipe dry.

9. *Degloss the old paint* by going over it with fine soapless steel wool or medium-grit sandpaper. Sandpaper is always easier to handle if you wrap a sheet of it around a wooden block or similar object.

10. *As you degloss*, watch for any rough areas on the surface. Smooth these with a few extra swipes with the sandpaper.

11. *Thoroughly vacuum* away all loose sanding dust and dirt.

PRIMER FOR TRIM

You won't need a primer for trim if the old paint is intact —and if it's a light color and you are planning to put a light color over it.

You will need to spot-prime over patches and on any areas where the bare wood is exposed. Assuming that you are going to be using semigloss or glossy paint or enamel, spot-prime with an enamel undercoater.

Prime the entire trim surface if you are going to be putting a light-colored paint over dark, or when putting any color paint over varnished wood. Use an enamel undercoater for priming. This material comes in white only, but can be tinted with universal tinting colors (available at all paint stores) to more closely approximate the color of the finish paint.

If the old trim surfaces are stained—by sap, dampness, or some unknown staining agent, and you want to block the stains from bleeding through the finish paint, prime with a coat of pigmented shellac sealer (also known as stain-killer).

Actually, because it dries so quickly and has such excellent bonding properties, pigmented shellac sealer is a good choice in many situations where a primer is required. Like enamel undercoaters, pigmented shellac sealer comes in white only, but can be tinted by mixing in universal tinting color in the appropriate shade.

Of course, whenever you are in doubt about whether to prime or not, and with what, check the label on the container of finish paint to see what the manufacturer recommends.

HOW TO PREPARE WATER-DAMAGED TRIM SURFACES

Because of leaks from the outside and/or moisture in the wood, new paint applied to sills and other trim surfaces around windows and some doors may be short-lived. Water that has somehow seeped into the wood causes the paint to flake off.

What to do about it? Use weatherstripping to make sure that there is a good tight seal around windows and doors when they are closed. There are several different kinds of weatherstripping materials. A visit to a well-stocked hardware store will give you an idea of what's available. Caulking compound may be another solution.

Whatever the source of the leak, get the problem taken care of first, or moisture will continue to dampen the wood and ultimately lift off the paint.

After the repair has been made, give the wood several days to dry out before painting it. Then prime with pigmented shellac sealer before applying the finish paint.

WHAT TO DO IF YOU WANT TO STRIP AND REFINISH PAINTED WOOD TRIM

You have painted trim now, but you'd prefer a natural wood look? Turn to Chapter X for information about how to use a chemical paint remover. Then finish the wood according to the step-by-step instructions for putting a clear finish on wood furniture (also in that same chapter).

But first a word of warning: It is one thing to strip and then refinish a single piece of furniture. Work, yes, but fun, if you like that sort of thing, and very often the results more than compensate for the time and energy expended.

Stripping all the woodwork in a room—or throughout the house—is a much bigger job, and the final results may be disappointing. Keep in mind that the wood might have been painted for a purpose; it could be that it just isn't handsome enough on its own. Unless you have some reason to suspect that the woodwork is of beautiful old oak or mahogany or some other attractive species, you may rue the day you ever decided to embark on the refinishing process.

HOW TO PREPARE NEW TRIM

New windows, or a new door, or any new wood surface must be primed before you paint it. But first go over the wood with sandpaper to get rid of any surface dirt and to smooth away roughness. Pay special attention to knots, if there are any, and to the areas around them.

Vacuum away the sanding dust. Then wipe the surface with a cloth saturated in mineral spirits. Wipe dry with a fresh cloth. If the wood is knotty, or if there are sap streaks in evidence, prime with a coat of pigmented shellac sealer. If there are no knots, and you are going to use a glossy or semigloss paint or enamel on the new trim, prime the wood with a coat of enamel undercoater. In either case, allow the primer to dry thoroughly before applying the finish paint.

HOW TO PROTECT WHAT YOU DON'T WANT PAINTED

As we've just pointed out, getting trim paint on walls is no big deal if the walls are still to be painted. But trim paint smeared on the floor, on windowpanes, or on adjacent surfaces that you do not intend to paint over is something else again.

True, fresh paint is relatively easy to clean away with a cloth dampened with water, or with mineral spirits, if you're using an alkyd paint, and these things should always be close at hand while you work. But pausing for occasional spot removal is a nuisance. It interrupts the main business at hand: applying a well-controlled coat of paint.

You can keep these interruptions to a minimum if you learn the techniques for keeping paint in its place.

1. *Masking tape.* One way to protect what you don't want painted is to cover its edges with masking tape. Ideally, strips of

tape should be applied straight and smooth so that they are flush against the edges of the trim surface to be painted. The exception is when you are painting a window sash, in which case the tape should be positioned on the panes between $\frac{1}{16}$ and $\frac{1}{8}$ of an inch away from the edges of the sash. That way, a hairline stripe of paint will be flowed onto the panes; a thin edging of paint here is desirable because it helps keep a tight seal in the puttied joint between panes and sash.

The amateur may find it difficult to lay the tape on in perfect position. Apply the tape too far from trim edges and the paint can smear over onto the surface you want to protect. Apply the tape too close and it can cover up part of the trim you want painted. Apply it too loosely and the paint can run under it. Leave the tape on for too long, and a gooey residue may be left behind when you pull it off. (This residue can be removed by wiping with rubbing alcohol and then scraping it off with a single-edge razor blade. But to be on the safe side, always remove masking tape as soon as the paint is dry.)

Masking tape shouldn't be used at all on wallpaper; there's always the possibility that some of the paper will tear away when you pull up the tape. It should be noted, too, that masking tape may take some of the finish paint along with it when it is removed.

All of this is not to say that masking tape is impossible to work with—only to warn you that it must be applied carefully and properly if it's to do any good.

2. *Paint shields.*   These are an alternative to masking tape—perhaps a better alternative for those whose natures are too impatient for the fussy precision work of laying down the tape. A paint shield is just a thin, flat strip of metal or plastic that you can buy at any hardware or paint store.

To use it, hold it in one hand so that its edge is flush against the edge of the trim to be painted. In this position it forms a barrier between trim and the surface you want to protect. Paint with the other hand. You must wipe the shield clean each time you move it to another section, or the paint that accumulates on

110

the front of the shield will leak over to the back and mess up the very surface you're trying to protect.

You could improvise paint shields with cardboard. If you do, make sure to have several strips handy. Cardboard is absorbent; paint soaks into it and can't be wiped away completely, so you'll need to switch to a fresh strip of cardboard whenever you see the beginnings of paint buildup on the one you're using.

3. *Painting freehand and the technique of "cutting in."* It's possible to paint neatly and cleanly along a trim edge without masking or using a shield. In fact, almost all professional painters do it with ease.

A few professionals and many amateurs use a small pad made especially for painting trim. The technique is to load the pad, then press it against the surface to be painted so that the edge of the pad lines up with the edge of the surface. The pad is then wiped smoothly and firmly in one direction only. Crucial here is that the edge of the pad be moved precisely along the edge of the trim surface.

Others prefer the technique of "cutting in" with a sash brush. In cutting in, it's important not to overload the brush. Dip just the first inch or so of bristles into the paint, then remove any excess by tapping the brush against the side of the paint container.

Now, let's say you want to paint cleanly along the edge of a doorframe where it meets the wall. Press the ends of the bristles firmly against the frame, close to but not touching the adjacent wall. Twist your wrist just enough to make the bristles start to fan out. Now, begin your brush stroke, gently and gradually "pushing" closer to the edge of the frame where it meets the wall. The slightly fanned bristles, combined with a firm but slow and steady stroke, give you the control needed to apply a neat, clean stripe of paint. Continue the stroke in one direction only until paint no longer flows freely off the brush. Reload, as above, and begin a new stroke.

Practice cutting in until you've mastered the knack. It's well worth learning and, once you've got the feel of it, not at all difficult.

HOW TO PAINT A DOOR

You'll need a narrow trim roller, brush, or small paint pad for edges and moldings and panels, and a wider brush, roller, or pad for the rest.

1. *Start* by painting the top edge and the two long vertical edges of the door.

But what if the two sides of the door are to be painted different colors? Which color do you paint the edges then?

Easy. The edge nearest the hinge should match trim in the room it faces when the door is open (the room that the door opens *out* of, in other words). The knob edge should match trim in the room *it* faces when the door is open (that's the room the door opens *into*). The top edge should match trim in the room the door opens into, if you care.

2. *To finish painting a flat or flush door* (one with no panels), simply use roller, brush, or pad as you would to apply paint to other large flat surfaces.

3. *If you're painting a paneled door*, start with the indented panels and the narrow moldings around them. Don't overload the applicator. You want good coverage, but you don't want paint to collect at the bottom corners of the panels. If you see this happening, go back and with light strokes redistribute the paint away from the corner.

Do the raised surfaces next; horizontals first, then verticals. Finish with long, light horizontal strokes with just the tips of the bristles for the horizontal surfaces; use long, light vertical strokes for the verticals. For a stroke-free finish, gradually lift the applicator at the end of each long, light stroke.

4. *Paint the inner part of the doorframe next.* If the two sides of the door are to be painted different colors, you may be puzzled about where to leave off painting with one color and start up with the other.

Let's say you are working on the side of the door that opens *out* of the room. In that case, paint all sections of the inner frame that are visible when the door is closed. (No, don't close the door at this point; you'll be able to tell which sections those are just by taking a good look.) The rest of the inner frame should be painted to match the other side of the door.

If you are working on the side of the door that opens *into* the room, paint up to—but not beyond—the door side of the doorstop. (The doorstop is the strip of molding against which the door closes.)

NOTE: The last two paragraphs may sound confusing if you read them without having a door in front of you for reference. But read them over again with a door nearby, and you'll get the idea immediately.

Paint the top of the inner frame first. Then bring paint down the sides.

5. *Finish by painting the outer surfaces of the frame.* Work across the top first, then down the sides. Use a narrow trim roller, sash brush, or small paint pad to cut along the edges where frame meets wall.

If you painted the door in place without removing it from its hinges, it should be left ajar. Don't open or close it until it is dry.

HOW TO PAINT BASEBOARDS

Except for the bending and stooping, baseboards are a snap to paint. Work in approximately three-foot-wide sections. Cut in carefully along the top edge where baseboard meets walls and the bottom where it meets floors. Or, use a paint shield or apply masking tape to protect walls and floors, as you prefer.

Paint the top edge of each section first. Use a narrow trim brush or sash brush or small paint pad here and to paint the bottom edge. Switch to a wider brush, roller, or paint pad for the vertical surfaces.

HOW TO PAINT WAINSCOTING
AND WOOD PANELING

To paint wainscoting or wood paneling, combine the techniques of painting baseboards with those of painting a paneled door. Work in manageable sections—three feet by three feet is convenient for most people. Paint from top to bottom within each section.

1. *Cut carefully along narrow edges* where wainscoting meets walls and floors. (Or use a shield or apply masking tape.)

2. *Paint the indented panels,* if any, and the molding around them. Use a trim brush or a small paint pad. If you see paint collecting in the bottom corners of the panels, go back and with light strokes redistribute the paint up and away from the corners.

3. *Do the raised surfaces.* Finish with long, light crosswise strokes on the horizontals, long, light, up-and-down strokes on the verticals. For smooth, even coverage, gradually lift the applicator at the end of each long stroke.

HOW TO PAINT WINDOWS

Basically, there are two kinds of windows: double-hung and casement. The sequences for painting them are different. But regardless of the kind of window in question, one of your primary concerns is to keep paint from being smeared onto the glass.

We noted previously that masking tape can be used to protect the glass, and this is just a reminder: If you do decide to use masking tape, apply it so that there is a hairline stripe of exposed glass between tape and sash. A sliver-fine edging of paint where glass and sash meet helps to keep the joint between them sealed.

For the same reason, if you use a shield, hold it almost but not quite flush against the sash. And if you paint freehand, with a sash brush, try to leave a fine line of paint on the glass along the sash. For the steady of hand, this is not nearly as difficult as it sounds.

In any case, to avoid a lot of time-consuming cleanup later on when the paint is dry and hard to remove, have a cloth handy (mineral spirits too, if you're using an alkyd paint) and keep an eagle eye out for smears. Wipe smears away promptly, as they occur.

Double-hung windows. These are the kind with two vertical sashes: an outer sash at the top, and an inner sash at the bottom. The outer sash can be lowered. The inner sash can be raised.

Some double-hung windows are made so that each sash can be lifted out. If this is the case with yours, then by all means remove them and lay them down for painting on a floor, table, or other large surface suitably protected with drop cloths or newspaper. That way, you won't have to go through the rigmarole of raising and lowering sashes described in the next few paragraphs. If your sashes can't be removed, or if it's too cold outside to live in a windowless room for the time it will take the sashes to dry, paint in the following sequence:

1. *Raise the inner sash* as far as possible. Lower the outer sash as far as possible. The idea is to expose the horizontal strip at the bottom of the outer sash. Paint this strip. Then paint as much as you can of the exposed muntins (if any) above it. Do the horizontals first, then the verticals.

115

(What are muntins? Where there are multiple panes of glass in the sash, muntins are the narrow strips dividing the panes and holding them secure within the sash.)

2. *Lower the inner sash* so that it is almost but not quite closed. Raise the outer sash almost but not quite all the way. With a sash brush, paint the muntins on the outer sash. Do the horizontals first, then the verticals.

Muntins are the hardest part of painting a window. Take it easy; don't rush the job. When you're finished with them, the worst will be over.

3. *With a trim brush or paint pad*, finish painting the outer sash. Do the horizontal pieces first, then the verticals.

4. *Paint the inner sash*—again, muntins first, if any—then the wider horizontal and vertical surfaces.

5. *Paint the inner part of the frame.* Do the horizontal surface at the top first, then bring paint down the sides. *Paint only those side sections of the inner frame that are visible when the window is completely closed.* (But don't close the window at this point; remember, it is already almost, but not quite, closed.)

Be careful when working along the edges where inner frame meets sash. Too much paint here and not only will the results look sloppy, but the window may also "freeze" into position.

6. *Paint the remainder of the frame.* Once again, do the horizontal top surface first, then paint down the sides.

7. *Paint the sill.* To make sure that the sashes don't dry frozen into position, raise and lower both a couple of inches three or four times while the paint is drying.

Casement windows. These are the kind of windows that swing in and out, usually by means of a crank or some other

116

device with moving parts. Don't paint the moving parts; otherwise you'll have a harder time getting the window to open and close.

1. *Open the window,* but not so far that you have to lean way out in order to reach it. With a sash brush, paint muntins, if any.

2. *Paint the top and bottom edges of the sash,* then the sides.

3. *Paint the inner part of the frame,* top first, then down each side.

4. *Paint the remainder of the frame,* again top first, then sides.

5. *Finish with the sill.*

HOW TO PAINT SHUTTERS

Use the same tools, and follow the same sequence given for painting a door: edges first (don't forget the bottom edge of each shutter); then panels, if any; then raised surfaces.

How to Paint Louvered Shutters

You can paint louvered shutters (doors, too) with a narrow trim brush or paint pad.

1. *Start with the edges of the frame* in which the louvers are set. Cut in on these edges along each individual louver. Then finish painting the edges.

2. *Starting with the top louver,* cut in at one end, then stroke paint toward the center, gradually lifting brush or pad as you

approach the midpoint. Cut in at the other end of the louver, and stroke paint toward the center, again lifting brush or pad as you approach the midpoint. Without reloading the applicator, finish the louver with light, long strokes across it. Working from top to bottom, paint each individual louver in this way.

NOTE: In painting from ends to center, as described, it will be easier to avoid a buildup of paint at one end than if you painted from end to end across each louver.

Every once in a while check to make sure that paint isn't spilling over onto the reverse side of the louvers. If you see any spillover, wipe it away immediately. (Keep a cloth and water or mineral spirits handy for this purpose.)

3. *To finish the louvered piece*, use a trim brush, roller, or small paint pad to do the edges—top, sides, and bottom. Then paint remaining flat surfaces, finishing with long, light crosswise strokes on horizontals; use long, light, up-and-down strokes on the verticals. For a smooth, even finish, gradually lift the applicator at the end of each long, light stroke.

Another way to paint louvered pieces is to spray them. Use a spray gun if you have one and know how to use it. Or, use cans of aerosol-spray paint. (The latter can be an expensive proposition if you have several pieces to paint, however, since each can holds only a very few ounces.)

When spray-painting, remember, it's extremely important to work in a well-ventilated room. Also, be careful to protect with drop cloths or newspaper everything you don't want painted. Of course, with a spray booth you would need to take fewer precautions. (You can improvise a spray booth by removing the front flaps from a cardboard carton tall enough and wide enough to enclose the piece you're painting. Stand the carton on its side, position the piece within it, then spray away, being careful not to overspray past the edges of the carton.)

If you are painting both sides of the piece, make sure the first side is dry before you turn it to paint the other side.

For more about spray-painting techniques, see Chapter III.

HOW TO PAINT BUILT-IN CABINETS
AND CUPBOARDS

We've said it before, but it's worth saying again: It's easier to remove knobs, pulls, handles, etc., than it is to paint around them. If you haven't already done so, unscrew hardware from built-in storage pieces and keep it all together in a coffee can or other container until time to replace it. Drawers and any shelves that aren't firmly attached to the piece should be removed and painted separately.

The hardest part about painting a built-in is reaching inside to get at interior surfaces. There's not much room for maneuvering, and unless you follow the proper sequence, you can end up paint-smeared from knuckles to elbow. Wielding a brush within confined spaces is easier if you saw off part of its handle—a trick employed by many pros. Painting in the following sequence will enable you to cover all surfaces systematically with a minimum of paint smeared on you.

1. *With a trim brush* (sawed off) or paint pad, paint the inside back wall of the piece.

2. *Paint the underside of the top* (or "roof") of the built-in. Then, starting with the top shelf and working down, do the undersides of all shelves.

3. *Paint the side walls.*

4. *Paint the tops of the shelves,* then their edges.

5. *If there are any narrow vertical strips* (stiles) separating the shelves, paint these and their edges.

6. *Paint all other exterior surfaces* (not including doors). Work from top to bottom. Don't forget the underside of the

piece, if it is exposed. For a smooth, even coating, finish with long, light strokes, gradually lifting the applicator at the end of each stroke.

7. *If you haven't removed the doors*, paint their inside surfaces first, then swing them partly closed and paint their exteriors. If the doors are paneled, see the section on how to paint paneled doors.

Don't close the doors all the way until the piece is completely dry.

8. *Paint only the front surfaces of the drawers.* Paint all surfaces of any doors that have been removed. Do not replace until paint is completely dry. Don't forget the bottom edges if they are visible when the doors are open.

VII

How to Paint Brick & Other Masonry

For this book, our definition of masonry includes brick and concrete, and also concrete and cement and cinder blocks, stone, tile, and stucco.

The very nature of masonry makes it different from other surfaces. Its components are earth substances. Bricks are kiln-baked blocks of clay. Concrete is stone, sand, and gravel, mixed with water. Mortar (the holding material between bricks or concrete blocks) is lime or cement mixed with sand and water. And so on.

You don't have to know much about masonry to see that it's durable. It doesn't *need* paint to protect it. With few exceptions, we paint masonry to make it look better or so it will be easier to keep clean—or because it needs waterproofing.

If you prefer a natural look rather than a painted surface, you may elect to put a transparent sealer on your masonry to protect it against stains. The preparation for the job, however, is much the same for applying a sealer as it is for applying paint. And at the risk of sounding repetitious, let's say again that with masonry, preparation is the larger part of the job.

SOME GENERAL INFORMATION
ABOUT PAINTING MASONRY

Before we tell you how to paint some different types of interior masonry, here are some general things to know about painting masonry:

1. *Don't rush in.*   To avoid disasters, don't rush in and paint new masonry as soon as it has set. Wait six months, or if you're in a hurry, six weeks, at least, before painting it. Even the mortar holding together a wall of bricks or concrete blocks needs time to "cure" or season. Particles of cement and sand that haven't been able to retain enough moisture to harden keep coming to the surface during the first few months. If you paint before the particles have had time to surface and be scrubbed away, you may be stuck with flaking and peeling paint—and, eventually, a lot more work!

2. *Scrub the unpainted surface.*   When painting new (but seasoned) masonry, or old masonry that hasn't been painted before, it's important to brush the surface vigorously with a stiff wire brush and scrub it down with strong detergent and water before you paint. A thorough vacuuming afterward, when it has dried (use the floor attachment of the vacuum cleaner) should rid the surface of any remaining fine loose particles. But don't vacuum until the larger pieces of matter have been brushed and scrubbed away.

3. *Wash the painted surface.*   When repainting masonry, if the paint is in good condition you shouldn't have any problems. Just wash the surface with a strong detergent and water first, then paint. Of course, if the previous paint is glossy, you'll have to sand it before repainting so the new coat of paint will stick to it.

If the previous paint is in good condition, but the surface is

122

grimy and there are oil and grease spots on it, scrub it with tri-sodium phosphate (TSP) and hot water. Use one cup of TSP per gallon of hot water. Or try a prepared degreaser, available in hardware and paint stores. Then rinse by swabbing the surface with clear water. If the paint is chalky, or flaking and peeling, you'll find what you need to know about repainting it in the "Problems" section of this chapter.

4. *Paint it damp.* Because most masonry is very porous and absorbs paint like a thirsty sponge, it's best to dampen the surface before painting. But always read the directions on the label of your can of paint to see if other methods should be followed.

WHAT PAINT TO USE

All those earth substances in masonry mean that it's loaded with alkali—which, as far as paint is concerned, means trouble. Alkali and ordinary paint are not exactly compatible, which is why it's important to use special alkali-resistant masonry paint. Alkali leech to the surface of the masonry and can be scrubbed away—but even if a wall is scrubbed free of alkali before it is painted, new moisture can bring more to the surface and cause the paint to flake and peel right off the wall. If you use alkali-resistant paint, there's a good chance of avoiding this. But there may still be problems. Masonry paints are "alkali-resistant," not "alkali-proof."

1. *Latex paints.* The most widely used and probably the best alkali-resistant paints for most purposes are latex paints formulated especially for use on masonry. These paints come in tough, glossy floor finishes as well as flat wall finishes and some are especially heavy-bodied and formulated for use on porous basement walls. Although ordinary latex wall paint does just fine on a brick wall that's in good condition, it won't do for all masonry. Before buying your paint, be sure to read the label thoroughly to make

sure you're getting what you need. If there's any doubt, check with your paint dealer.

Latex masonry paints are most easily applied with a long-napped roller, but they can be sprayed or brushed on as well. They are not recommended for painting cinder and slag, however, which require a rubber-base paint.

2. *Alkyd paints.* There are also a number of alkyd paints reinforced with resins to make them alkali-resistant. They're most often used for painting stucco, but are not recommended for new masonry or for surfaces that may become damp. When using alkyds on stucco, the surface should be completely *dry* before it is painted. (See the section on painting stucco at the end of this chapter.)

3. *Epoxy paints.* These paints are not alkyds or latexes but are purely chemical formulations recommended for use where there is the most wear and tear as well as moisture. They are especially recommended for painting tile and glazed bricks. They come in two containers; the contents must be mixed together before use, and the paint is difficult to apply, particularly because it dries so quickly. But they wear like iron. Epoxies are applied most effectively with a spray gun or a brush, but clean up with the special epoxy thinner immediately after painting or you'll never be able to use your equipment again. In fact, you could plan on *not* using the equipment again, and save yourself some heartache. Always follow the directions on the label closely and carefully, and work with windows and doors open for ventilation. And since the paint dries so quickly, do not let anything or anybody interrupt you until after you've finished cleaning up.

Epoxies will not adhere to other paints, but they will go on over old epoxies or over unpainted masonry.

4. *Cement paints.* These are heavy-bodied paints, sometimes called Portland cement paints. They come in dry powder form and must be mixed with water. They are actually composed

mostly of cement, which is about two thirds of their total composition. Once they were widely used, but with the development of alkali-resistant latex masonry paints their popularity has dwindled. They are, however, especially recommended for use on masonry that is extremely porous and rough and/or marred with small cracks, which they will fill and cover. They are never recommended for use on floors because they never quite harden, even when dry.

Cement paints are best applied with a pliable-fiber brush and scrubbed into the dampened masonry surface. They will not adhere to other paints and should be applied only to unpainted masonry.

5. *Rubber-base paints.* These contain synthetic rubber solids and are alkali-resistant, skid-proof, and moisture-proof as well. They take a good deal of wear and abrasion and are recommended for basement floors, masonry stairs, etc. Because of their moisture-proof qualities, they are also recommended for basement walls.

6. *Masonry primer-fillers.* These are special primers (such as Primafil) containing fillers for use on very rough and porous masonry—particularly certain types of concrete blocks—that is particularly difficult to paint. They brush on to yield a smoother surface for the application of paint.

7. *Masonry sealers and conditioners.* These come in three varieties:

- Clear sealers that soak into the masonry and protect it from stains and later make it easier to clean.

- Pigmented, rubber-base, epoxy-fortified waterproofing sealers that, when applied correctly to unpainted masonry, are guaranteed to make it watertight.

- Conditioners, or surface coatings, that can be applied to unpainted masonry to seal and harden the surface and lessen the chance of paint failure. They can also be used to seal up a dusty, chalky, previously painted surface before the application of new paint. (Thoro-Seal is one such conditioner.)

THE APPLICATION OF THE PAINT

The quickest and easiest way to paint most masonry is with a roller that has a nap of at least ½ inch or longer. Roll slowly so the roller can work its way into the surface. When painting a floor or other flat surface, pour on the paint and then roll it out with an extended roller. On floors, pour out about a pint of paint at a time, roll it out, and then blend in successive patches.

If you prefer a brush to a roller, buy a large whitewash brush. The roughness of the masonry will wear out a better brush too quickly.

When using cement paint, always apply it with a brush.

SOME PROBLEMS THAT MAY COME UP

1. *Efflorescence* is an alkali-related problem of masonry. It is a whitish, powdery haze or stain that appears in spots on brick or concrete when there's more than a bit of moisture in the air. What happens is that the moisture leeches out the salts created by the alkali in the masonry. While this may or may not be an eyesore, you'll have to remove it if you plan to paint the masonry. Paint won't stick to efflorescence.

Efflorescence can be scrubbed away with muriatic acid and water and a good, stiff scrub brush. *But always take precautions when using muriatic acid. It's a strong and dangerous chemical. Always wear rubber gloves and eye protection (glasses or goggles) and read the directions on the container carefully before you begin.* Here's a three-step guide for working with muriatic acid:

126

- Pour a quart of water into a plastic bucket and then add one cup of muriatic acid to it. (Always add the muriatic acid to the water instead of vice versa.)

- Using the scrub brush, swab the solution on the efflorescence to dissolve it. Then rinse it off completely with clear water.

- Paint the surface within four hours—before new efflorescence has a chance to form.

2. *Is the surface too rough or too smooth?* Either way, there'll be problems. If you're painting a concrete floor or steps that are extremely smooth, the paint may not stick to the surface. You'll have to roughen the concrete a bit to give it sufficient "tooth" for the paint to adhere. Scrubbing the concrete with muriatic acid and water should etch it enough so it will hold the paint. Follow the directions given above for using muriatic acid.

If, on the other hand, the masonry you want to paint seems too heavily textured with deep pores, it may also be difficult to paint, as it will take an excess of time and paint (gallons!) to cover it effectively. Coat the surface with a latex masonry primer-filler (such as Primafil) that will fill in the pores and yield a smoother surface on which to apply the top coat or two of paint.

3. *On previously painted masonry,* if the old paint is *chalking,* the surface should be cleaned with strong detergent and water and then coated with a masonry surface conditioner to seal and harden it before painting. This should eliminate further chalking.

If the old paint is *flaking and peeling,* it's best to remove as much of the old paint as possible—preferably all of it—before applying the new. There's a reason for such seeming madness. By removing the old failed paint right down to the bare masonry, you may be able to remove the cause of the paint failure as well. Unfortunately, the only way to do a thorough job of paint removal is by sandblasting. It's not a job I'd do myself. The equipment is complicated to use—that is, if you can find someone who'll rent it to you. Instead, I'd look in the Yellow Pages for a good professional sandblaster and get the job over and done with. Then, vacuum the surface and coat it with a masonry conditioner. The conditioner will seal and harden the surface which, after the sandblasting, will be soft and dusty.

It may be possible to do a decent job without sandblasting, however, though it will be time-consuming and tedious work. First, scrub away as much of the loose paint as possible with a wire brush or a wire power brush rented from your hardware dealer. Follow this with an application of a good semipaste paint remover applied according to the directions and safety precautions on the container. Be sure to apply the paint remover by slapping it on in thick layers and stroking in one direction only, and work on small sections at a time. Follow by washing the surface with a strong detergent and water, rinsing, and repeating the application of paint remover two or three times if necessary. (Sandblasting, especially if someone else does it for you, certainly is easier!)

Important: If you're repainting old masonry that you suspect has been coated with either calcimine or whitewash, don't try to paint over it without removing the old finish—even though it seems to be in good condition. Neither calcimine nor whitewash will take new paint!

You can remove calcimine by washing it with strong detergent and warm water. But to remove whitewash, you'll have to use a hand sander or an electric sander. Then wash the surface with detergent and water, and prime it with a masonry conditioner before repainting. You could, of course, just clean off the old whitewash and cover it with another coat of whitewash—but nobody's doing that these days. There are better paints around!

4. *Filling in cracks.* To fill in cracks—and small holes as well—use a vinyl concrete-patching cement (available in paint stores and hardware stores) and a finely pointed trowel. If the cracks seem too fine to fill, they'll probably disappear if you paint

the surface with a heavy-bodied latex masonry paint of the type formulated for use on basement walls. Or use a cement paint.

5. *Repairing loose mortar.*   Before painting brick, block, or stone, you'll want to fix any loose joints with mortar cement. This is available in paint and hardware stores as a prepackaged mix; all you do is add water according to the directions on the box and go to work. The job boils down to six steps:

- Scrape out the old mortar to a depth of about ½ inch. You'll need a small chisel to do this. Work gently, using the corner of the blade to scrape away the old mortar, and instead of working away the full ½ inch in one sweep, do it in shallow sweeps. If you're working on a brick wall, be careful not to get the chisel too far between the bricks or you run the risk of splitting them. Work one section at a time, and only where necessary.

- Using a stiff brush, clean away all loose material and dust from the joint.

- Splash some water on the area with a brush or a sponge so it is damp when you apply fresh mortar.

- Mix the mortar thoroughly, dampen the area again, and pack the mortar in firmly with the tip of a small triangular pointing trowel.

- As soon as the mortar begins to stiffen, finish it off so it looks like the other joints in the wall.

- Clean the excess mortar off the surface before it dries by scraping with your trowel or using a stiff brush dipped in water.

If there are cracks in the brick, etc., use the same mortar cement and trowel to fill them in. Then let the mortar cure for at least two weeks before you paint, keeping it damp for at least 48 hours after the application of the mortar.

HOW TO PAINT DIFFERENT TYPES OF MASONRY

1. *Brick.* If the brick has never been painted before, but is very dirty (if, for example, you've just exposed a potentially beautiful old brick wall), go over it vigorously with a wire brush to remove all loose plaster, dirt, and debris—or use a rented wire power brush to do the job. Then scrub with strong detergent and water. Rinse away the detergent, then paint. If the brick is in good shape, forgo the wire brushing and just wash it. If there is efflorescence, however, clean the brick with muriatic acid and water, following all the precautions for working with muriatic acid described on page 126. Then rinse with clear water.

Repair any loose joints with mortar cement as described above, and wait at least two weeks for the mortar to set before painting.

To keep the *natural* look of the brick and still protect it from soiling, brush or roll on two coats of a transparent masonry sealer. As brick is quite porous, be prepared to use a good bit of the sealer.

If you decide to paint the brick, the easiest paint to use is latex interior wall paint applied with a long-napped roller. If you've just repaired the mortar, however, use an alkali-resistant latex masonry paint. You'll probably need two coats of paint—and, again, don't expect to get the same coverage you would on a smooth, nonporous surface.

If the brick has been painted before and the paint is in good condition, just wash it with a strong detergent and water, rinse with clear water, and then paint. If the paint is peeling and flaking, however, it's best to remove all the paint down to the bare brick, according to directions given in the "Problems" section of this chapter, before painting.

2. *Ceramic tile and glazed brick.* If you've inherited puce

ceramic tile in your bathroom or shower stall, or glazed brick of indeterminate color in your kitchen, there's hope yet. Both can be painted the same way. First wash with a strong detergent and water, then cover the surface completely with a paste made of powdered pumice and water and rub it in with a cloth. (You can buy powdered pumice at most hardware stores.) This will roughen the surface and will remove any film left by the detergent. Or from soap. Be especially careful to pumice the areas around soap dishes. Then rinse and let dry.

To paint, brush on a good epoxy paint, even though it may be difficult to apply. If you follow the directions on the label to a T, you'll have a glossy, moisture-resistant finish that could look better than new. Don't let anything interrupt you as you work, however. Don't even stop to answer the phone. The paint dries quickly. Clean up any drips and spatters immediately with special epoxy thinner, but you might as well plan on throwing away any brushes you use. You'll never get them clean. Once epoxy paint starts hardening, it doesn't stop until it's like a rock.

If a water-resistant, wear-resistant coating isn't necessary— if, for example, the tile or bricks are in a little-used area away from water—epoxy paint won't be necessary. First clean and pumice the tiles or bricks, then coat them with a pigmented shellac-base primer (such as B-I-N or Enamelac). This primer will bond securely and will produce a surface over which you can apply any paint you want. Shellac-base primers can be thinned with denatured alcohol, which is also used for the cleanup. The surface should be dry enough for the application of the top coat within forty-five minutes.

3. *Cinder blocks.* We don't know where you'd have cinder blocks indoors, except in the cellar or the garage. If you do have them, it's possible to paint them. But cinder blocks often contain particles of iron that bleed through or react with latex paints. The surface is often quite rough as well. For these reasons, the paint job can be tricky. It's best to use a rubber-base paint, ap-

plied with a roller that has a long nap. And roll slowly, so the nap can work into the surface and give good paint coverage. Several coats of paint may be necessary.

4. *Concrete.* If possible, new concrete shouldn't be painted until it's six months old. It should be scrubbed with detergent and water and, if it's very dirty, with trisodium phosphate (TSP) and water. Then vacuum it. Any efflorescence should be removed with muriatic acid. Loose paint should be scraped off with a wire brush or, if necessary, a power brush or sander. Any holes and cracks should be patched with mortar. If the concrete is very porous, it can be filled in with a masonry primer-filler, which is sometimes also called a block filler. This is an optional step, but it does give you a smoother surface on which to paint. Then apply two coats of latex masonry paint, or rubber-base paint, or epoxy paint, depending on the finish you want, the moisture conditions, and how ambitious you are. If you want a clear finish, use a masonry sealer that soaks into the pores and prevents staining.

If a concrete floor is oily and greasy as well as dirty, and if TSP does not clean it adequately, try scrubbing with a special concrete floor degreaser of the kind used in gas stations (and often sold in them as well). If the concrete floor is hard-troweled and extremely smooth, etch it with muriatic acid before painting so it will have the necessary "tooth" to hold paint. When painting a floor, use an extended roller and make sure the roller has a nap that is at least ½-inch long. Pour the paint directly on the floor, about a pint at a time, and smooth it out with the roller, blending the sanded patches as you go. Be sure to smooth the paint out enough so you don't apply too thick a coat. Two thin coats are better than one thick one. Let each coat dry completely and sand each coat lightly before applying the next. Latex floor enamels or rubber-base floor enamels are recommended for basement floors, while epoxies or urethane floor enamels are recommended for concrete garage floors.

5. *Concrete blocks.* Concrete blocks can be painted in the same way as concrete, but they are usually much rougher and more porous. Instead of etching, they almost invariably could use priming with a filler, though this treatment is optional. First, however, repair any loose mortar. And if there is water seepage, plug up any active leaks by troweling in some ready-mixed "plug," which you can buy in a hardware store. Follow the directions on the container. Where there have been leaks or moisture damage, apply a waterproofing sealer and a water-resistant paint (such as a latex cement paint or a rubber-base paint) to the walls. If the concrete blocks have been painted before and the paint is peeling and flaking, remove as much of it as possible—all, if you can—before going further. (See page 126 for handling problems on masonry.)

6. *Flagstone and slate.* Flagstone and slate floors are rarely painted (we certainly don't recommend it), but they can be brushed with a clear masonry sealer to make them stain-resistant and easier to clean. All wax and dirt should be cleaned off the floor by washing with a strong detergent and water before the sealer goes on.

7. *Stone.* Interior stone can also be coated with a clear masonry sealer to help keep it clean and stain-free.

8. *Stucco.* Stucco is a porous concrete plaster. Ideally, it needn't be painted, although a sealer should be brushed on to protect it from stains. However, people do paint stucco. Before it's painted, it should be cleaned, with special attention paid to wiping the water out of the deeper depressions. (If the water isn't wiped out, it will stagnate if you don't paint immediately—and it might ruin your paint job even if you do paint right away.) Small holes and cracks can be repaired with a finely pointed trowel and a stucco-patching mixture that you can buy ready-mixed at most well-stocked hardware stores. The patches should

133

be dry before you paint. If the stucco has been painted before, you can brush on an alkyd masonry paint or a latex masonry paint. If you are painting the stucco for the first time, use the latex paint. See that the paint doesn't accumulate in the depressions.

VIII

How to Paint Metal

Painting metal is no harder and no easier than painting any other type of surface, but it does take work. As usual, preparation is 90 percent of the work. On second thought, make that 95 percent.

In general, and at the risk of oversimplifying, let's boil the job down to four steps:

- Cleaning the surface so it's free of oil, wax, grease, and dirt.

- Removing any rust and/or chipped, cracked, and peeling paint from the surface.

- Priming the surface with a rust-inhibiting primer made especially for use on metals.

- The actual paint job.

We'll go into the details of painting specific metals in a minute. But just so you know what we're talking about, let's describe these four steps a bit further.

1. *Cleaning the surface.* This is probably the most impor-

135

tant bit of preparation you'll do, and it could mean the difference between success or failure in the paint job.

But cleaning metal doesn't mean simply going over it with soap and water and a sponge. The surface must be free of oil, wax, and grease so that the paint will stick to it. Even new metal, fresh from the mill, should be cleaned before it's primed and painted, because all new metal is covered with an oily film to protect it from rust while it's being transported.

Most metals, including those that have already been painted, can be cleaned by wiping them quickly and thoroughly with mineral spirits (paint thinner) and a rag. However, when you're working in the kitchen, where you have your stove, or anywhere else where there's danger of combustion, we suggest cleaning metal with trisodium phosphate (available as TSP in paint and hardware stores) and water. Use one cup of TSP per gallon of warm water, and use according to directions on the container.

When you do use mineral spirits, work in a well-ventilated room with the windows open and be sure not to smoke. Mineral spirits are flammable. Be sure to dispose of all your saturated rags by placing them in a water-filled container along with a note telling your garbage collector what they are. Also wear rubber or plastic gloves when you work.

2. *Removing rust, chipped and peeling paint, etc.* Indoors, you usually don't find much rust on metal—unless you have a damp basement, or there's excessive moisture in the air, or you're painting metal that has been outdoors a while.

If there *is* rust, however, you must remove it before you paint. If you go ahead and paint right over rust, figuring you'll save yourself some work, you will be causing more work for yourself instead of less. The rust will just continue to grow under and through that nice new coat of paint.

Instead, vigorously go over the rusty spots with a medium or coarse grade of sandpaper or steel wool or a wire brush. And when you're removing rust from metal that has already been painted, go right down to the bare metal. (You won't hurt it!)

If there's a lot of rust on the metal, you might want to use a chemical rust remover (sanding the area after the chemicals have dried), or a power sander. Feather the edges of the area so there's no telltale line on the existing paint. If the paint is peeling as well, use a wire brush to scrape it away. Smooth the areas where paint may have chipped by rubbing them with sandpaper. If you have any trouble manipulating the sandpaper, dampen it and then rub. Or buy an emery cloth (at almost any hardware store) to do the sanding.

If there are dents in the metal, fill them in with a good metal filler, which you can buy in a hardware store or a paint store. Then sand over the filler once it's dry and prime it before you paint.

And here again is the same important step that has come up before. When you're repainting previously painted metal, if the existing paint is glossy, and it often is, you must degloss the finish by rubbing it with a medium grade of sandpaper so the new coat of paint will stick to it. Otherwise, the new paint could just slip right off. (It happens!)

3. *Priming the surface.* If you're working on previously painted metal and you've sanded away some rust, prime the exposed areas. Use the same rust-inhibiting primer you'd use if you were priming new or unpainted metal. It figures; once you've cleaned away the rust, you should be down to bare metal, which must always be primed before painting, whether it's new or old and weathered.

There are two important reasons for using primers on metal:

- To protect the metal from moisture and oxygen and the resulting rust and corrosion.

- To give you a better surface for the application of paint. The primer sticks to the metal; the paint sticks to the primer. Unless you're willing to experiment for yourself, take it on faith.

137

Important: Before you buy your metal primer, select the paint you want to use for the top coat and read the label thoroughly to see what primer the manufacturer recommends. For the best results, buy the primer that's recommended to be used with the top coat. Manufacturers go to great lengths to make primers and top coats that are compatible with each other.

Basically, there are two kinds of metal primers: zinc-chromate primers, which are white, for use on metals that aren't exposed to much moisture; and damp-proof red primers for metals that *are* exposed to moisture. If you're painting the pipes in your basement, it's a good idea to use a damp-proof red primer.

If you want, you can tint (or ask your paint dealer to tint) the white zinc-chromate primer with some universal color or a little of the top-coat paint you're going to use, so it is closer to the color of your top coat. That way, you may be able to get by using only one coat of top-coat paint.

After priming the metal, give the primer enough time to dry thoroughly before applying the top coat. (The label on the can of primer should tell you how long it will take to dry under specific conditions.)

4. *Painting the metal.* For most indoor uses, just about any paint that's compatible with your primer will effectively cover properly primed metal; this means any paint that fits in with your decorating scheme—latex paint or alkyd paint, in a flat, semigloss, or high-gloss finish. However, for surfaces that get much wear and tear, a high-gloss alkyd paint is usually recommended. And if you're painting a radiator or heating pipes, alkyd paints are again recommended because they are better able to withstand the heat.

Several manufacturers make a rust-inhibiting paint that has a primer built in so that you can prime and paint in one operation. Other manufacturers put all the rust inhibitors in the primer and sell a top coat to go with it that is, basically, alkyd enamel. Just to make sure that you know what you're getting and that you don't duplicate your steps, be sure to read the label on the can of top coat thoroughly.

5. *The application of the paint.* Metal is most effectively painted by brushing the paint on with a good bristle brush or by spraying it on—either from a can of spray paint or with spray equipment. (For all you need to know about spray paint, see Chapter III.) If you do spray-paint, take the object you're painting out to the garage or down to your unfinished basement and do the job there. Or protect everything else in the room with newspapers and drop cloths. And we do mean everything! Otherwise, you're bound to find evidence of overspray—in the form of tiny paint specks—wherever you look. If you really do want to spray-paint, and it's impossible to move the object out of the house, and you're not sure you can cover everything with drop cloths, you can devise a spraying booth out of corrugated cartons as described on page 66.

No matter what method you use to apply the paint, be sure to remove all removable hardware from cabinets and appliances and cover the hardware that isn't removable with masking tape. But be sure to remove the masking tape as soon as the paint is dry because masking tape is often quite difficult to remove later on. Many experienced painters forgo using the masking tape and apply a thick coating of petroleum jelly or another lubricant to the hardware so that the paint will not adhere to it.

When you spray-paint, it's best to apply two or three thin coats of paint rather than one thick coat. A thick coat of spray paint has a tendency to drip and sag and look unsightly once it has dried. And spray evenly across the surface, without lingering at any spot overly long. This, too, makes for dripping and sagging paint.

When brushing on enamel (which is the finish most frequently used on metal), take pains to apply the coating in a not-too-thin, not-too-thick film. Use a good quality enamel brush with a chisel tip, not a blunt tip. Load your brush with a bit more enamel than you would use if you were applying ordinary paint. And let it flow on without spreading it out too much. Always use light pressure; the bristles should hardly bend. Work in smallish sections. If you see any runs or sags or globs developing, go back immediately and redistribute the enamel by stroking it lightly and evenly away from the problem. Do this right away, before the enamel has a chance to dry and the glob becomes a permanent part of the surface.

If you don't feel comfortable applying the paint with a brush and want to use a paint pad or a roller instead, think twice about using either tool to apply semigloss or high-gloss coatings. Chances are you'll get a stippled effect instead of a nice smooth finish.

If you're painting columns or pipes or railings, or the legs of metal or wrought-iron furniture, you might want to use a painter's mitt to make the job easier. The mitt fits on your hand like a mitten and is made of nappy material much like that on a paint roller. Just dip the mitt into the paint and rub it on the surface, molding it around the object you're painting. (If you're using alkyd paint or a paint containing epoxies, throw the mitt away when you're finished rather than trying—in vain—to get it clean.)

If you're brushing or spraying on a high-gloss enamel and decide that a second coat is necessary, let the first coat dry thoroughly and then sand it so that the second coat will adhere well. (The manufacturers of some "instant" spray paint, however, advise applying the second and third thin coats of paint within three to four minutes of the application of the previous coat—with no sanding between coats.)

PAINTING SPECIFIC METALS AND SPECIFIC OBJECTS

Aluminum—including the aluminum around storm windows. Generally, indoors, aluminum doesn't have to be painted. If it is dirty and badly discolored, try wiping it down with a metal conditioner that contains phosphoric acid (available in paint and hardware stores) and steel wool, following directions on the container, until the surface is bright and new-looking.

If you do want to paint the aluminum, however, first wipe it down with mineral spirits. Then remove any rust with coarse sandpaper or steel wool or a wire brush—and, if it is new, sand the entire surface so the primer will adhere. You can use any metal primer or a primer made especially for aluminum. Then paint. For the top coat—and two coats of paint may be necessary— use any latex or alkyd paint that is compatible with your primer. If you want to keep a metallic look, try using an aluminized paint. (But be aware that it is difficult to paint over aluminized paint. You may have to use paint remover before repainting next time.)

If the aluminum has already been painted and the paint is peeling and there is rust, first clean the aluminum, then remove the rust and peeling paint with sandpaper and a wire brush, sand the entire surface lightly so the new paint will adhere, spot-prime the exposed areas, and *then* paint. If, however, the paint is in good shape, just clean the surface and sand it lightly before painting.

If you want to preserve a clear finish on bare aluminum, use a clear, non-yellowing acrylic lacquer. First wipe the surface with mineral spirits and sand it lightly, then brush on the lacquer— two coats if necessary. To remove old lacquer, use lacquer thinner and steel wool.

Appliances and metal cabinets. With all the cans of spray paint on the market especially packaged for spray-painting appliances, it is tempting to . . . well, spray-paint large kitchen appliances like refrigerators. I would think twice about it, however. Unless you're really good at wielding a spray can, you're bound to end up with a terrific case of overspray. Tiny specks of paint all over the windows, the lighting fixtures, the ceiling . . . whatever you haven't been able to cover with newspapers or tape or a drop cloth. Go ahead and spray if you want, but don't say we didn't warn you. If possible, make a spraying booth out of an old carton, as described on page 66.

Portable metal cabinets—file cabinets, storage cabinets, etc.—are another matter. Those you can take down to the basement or out to the garage and spray (if, of course, you have a basement or a garage). For information on spray painting, see Chapter III. But spray-painting stationary cabinets and large appliances, no. We recommend painting them by brushing the paint on. With the best brushes you can afford and the best semigloss alkyd enamel (for the cabinets) or epoxy enamel (for the appliances) you can find. And don't worry about brush marks. If your paint is really good, the brush marks should smooth right out.

Before painting, unscrew knobs, handles, hinges, etc., and keep them all together, in a tin can or a paper bag, along with the screws, until it's time to put them back again. Or cover the hardware with masking tape, being sure to remove the tape as soon as the paint is dry. Or you can cover the hardware with petroleum jelly so the paint will not stick to it. Remove the drawers and doors (if possible) and lift out any removable shelves and set them on several thicknesses of newspaper on the floor so they can be painted separately.

Then make sure the surface is free of dirt, grease, and polish. Clean kitchen cabinets and appliances with trisodium phosphate (TSP) and water. Use one cup of TSP per gallon of hot water. A super-saturated TSP solution—as much TSP as the water will hold so that no more powder will dissolve in it—will also degloss the surface. But be extremely careful when using TSP this way. It's very caustic. Wear rubber or plastic gloves and goggles to protect your eyes and be sure you have adequate ventilation.

Better to degloss the surface by sanding it once-over-lightly with sandpaper. It's not necessary to sand down to the bare metal, but only enough to roughen the surface sufficiently so that the new coat of paint will adhere.

If there is rust on the metal, sand it away with medium-grade sandpaper, feather the edges so they blend in with the intact finish, and spot-prime with metal primer. Then paint, applying several thin coats of paint rather than one thick coat. Let each coat dry thoroughly and then sand it lightly before applying the next coat.

When painting any cabinet, do the interior surfaces before the exteriors. Otherwise you take the chance of smudging a freshly painted exterior (and yourself as well) when you reach in to do the inside.

When doing the exteriors of portable cabinets, lift and turn the cabinet, if possible, so that the important large surfaces are in a horizontal position when you paint them; you'll avoid drips and sags. If the underside needs painting, turn the piece upside down and do the bottom first.

If you're painting cabinets in your bathroom, you can clean them with TSP and water as you would the kitchen cabinets, or with mineral spirits (paint thinner), taking all necessary precautions. After the surface is clean, remove any rust spots, spot-prime, sand once-over-lightly, and then paint. When you paint a medicine cabinet over the sink, be sure to put a drop cloth over the sink so the paint won't drip onto it.

Chrome. If the chrome is badly scratched or chipped and scraped away, clean it thoroughly with mineral spirits or TSP, remove any rust with coarse sandpaper, sand the entire surface lightly and prime it with a metal primer. Then paint with a chrome-finish aluminum paint.

Laundry driers. If the drier has the same porcelain enamel finish on all sides, clean it thoroughly according to the directions given for painting appliances on page 142. Sand it once-over-lightly and apply an epoxy enamel. If only the top is finished in porcelain enamel and the sides are of a less durable baked finish, paint the top as just directed. Then wash and sand the sides and paint them with an enamel formulated for use on metal.

If the top is chipped but otherwise in good condition, just touch up the chips with an epoxy touch-up enamel, applied according to the directions on the container.

Heating pipes.   If at all possible, don't paint heating pipes. Whatever paint you use will cause some heat loss.

If you must paint them, don't paint them when they're in use. Let them cool first—or wait until spring when the heat is turned off. Dust them and clean them with TSP and water. Remove any loose or peeling paint with a wire brush and sand away any rust. Then prime the pipes with a damp-proof red primer and paint with a high-gloss alkyd enamel formulated for use on metal. Latex paints will just peel off with the heat.

If you're painting heating pipes so you can identify them when necessary, red is the color to use. Otherwise, use any color that fits in with your decor.

Kitchen stoves and ranges.   It's best not to paint the stove or range. No matter how good a job you do, the new finish won't last long. If there are unsightly chips and bruises in the finish, clean them with detergent and water and then touch them up with epoxy touch-up enamel.

Metal furniture.   Clean metal furniture with mineral spirits and remove any rust with coarse sandpaper or an emery cloth. If the furniture has never been painted, sand the surface lightly all over and prime it with a metal primer. If it has been painted before, degloss the existing paint and spot-prime if necessary. Then paint with any paint that is compatible with your primer.

Metal tile.   Scrub the tile with detergent and water and clean any stains from the grout with scouring powder and steel wool. Or apply toothpaste to the grout to clean it. Let the toothpaste set for about fifteen minutes and then scrub it away with hot water and a scrub brush. Let the surface dry and then sand it lightly, prime it with an epoxy primer, and finish with epoxy enamel.

Radiators.   Never paint radiators when they're hot—which

144

means that the best time to paint them is during the late spring, summer, or early fall when they're not in use. Clean the entire surface with TSP and water and a scrub brush and use a special radiator cleaning brush to reach into the inner surfaces. Completely remove any loose or peeling paint with a wire brush or a power sander. Sand away any rust. If rust is a real problem, prime the radiator with a damp-proof red primer. If rust is not a big problem, use any rust-inhibiting metal primer. Paint with a good high-gloss alkyd enamel, which is the type of paint recommended for minimum heat loss. Latex paints will peel right off with the heat, so be sure not to use them. Use a long-handled, long-bristled brush to get into the hard-to-get-at places. It's a good idea to paint those first.

The best way to paint a radiator is to disconnect it and pull it out from the wall, then take it down to the basement and spray-paint it. We've never known anyone plucky enough to do this, however. Steam radiators can be disconnected by closing the shut-off valve and loosening the large nut with a pipe wrench, we're told. Hot-water radiators should be drained before they're disconnected. (Frankly, at this point I think I would call the plumbing and heating people.)

If the radiator has been painted before and the paint is in good condition, you can apply the new paint right over the old. If the radiator has been painted with an aluminized paint (which is not recommended as it causes a good deal of heat loss), use a power sander to remove the paint. Then wipe the radiator clean and prime and paint it with a high-gloss enamel.

New radiators must always be wiped down thoroughly with mineral spirits before priming.

Refrigerators. If there are only a few chips on the surface of the refrigerator, clean them with detergent and water, sand them and then touch them up with an epoxy touch-up enamel. If, however, an overall job is necessary, follow the directions given in the appliances part of this section. If your refrigerator

145

is not really ancient, it's unlikely that you will need to paint the interior. Most refrigerator interiors these days are made of hard plastic.

Tin.   Rub the tin with steel wool to subdue the shine, then apply an alkyd primer followed by a compatible alkyd enamel. If the tin is near a source of water, use an epoxy enamel.

Water pipes.   Never paint water pipes when they're moist and sweating. In fact, if they do sweat, any paint you apply could just peel right off and not be worth putting on. If you want to paint them anyway, make sure they're good and dry before you do, or the paint won't stick. First clean the pipes with mineral spirits and a rag. Remove any rust with coarse sandpaper or a power sander or a chemical rust-remover. (If you've used a chemical rust-remover, let the remover dry and then sand over the area.) If the pipes have been painted before, remove any loose or peeling paint by scrubbing vigorously with a wire brush or a power sander. Then prime the pipes with a damp-proof red primer—and if rust is a real problem, apply two coats of the primer, followed by a coat of a zinc-chromate primer. Then apply any compatible top coat, which could be one of the flat latex wall paints. Apply several coats of top coat if necessary.

Wrought iron.   Wipe off the wrought iron with paint thinner, then sand the surface lightly with sandpaper or steel wool. Apply a metal primer and a compatible top coat.

IX

How to Finish &
Refinish Floors

Finishing and refinishing wood floors used to be tedious, time-consuming, for-professionals-only work.

It's still time-consuming, though it may take half the time it used to, way back when. Some of the tedium has been taken out of the job and the paint manufacturers are coming out with easier-to-apply, faster-drying floor finishes every year. So, if you're willing to take the time and follow step-by-step instructions, it's possible to do a good job on your floors even if you've never done it before.

NOTE: It seems a good idea to mention this now: If you're painting your rooms as well as finishing or refinishing the floors, do the floors first. A lot of sanding dust will probably be flying around the room and you don't want it to land on your beautiful, freshly painted, not-quite-dry walls!

OUR RECOMMENDATION

There are several ways of finishing wood floors. When you're doing a complete finishing or refinishing job, you must first sand the floor (even if it's new) with a big drum sander which you can rent from a hardware dealer or a paint dealer or from a tool-rental agency. (Look in the Yellow Pages to find one, or ask for a recommendation from someone who has been through this.) After that, you can stain the wood darker than it is, or you can leave it just as it is. And you can finish it with several coats of a clear varnish-like finish or apply a penetrating sealer.

Since our objective is to do the job as simply and as easily as possible, we prefer the penetrating sealers to other finishes. You can simply wipe them on with a lint-free cloth, let them set for fifteen minutes or half an hour (according to the directions on the container), and then wipe off the excess. A second coat can go on the next day—or whenever the label on the can says to apply it. If you want your floors stained a darker color, there's no need to make the staining a separate operation. Some manufacturers (such as Minwax) package penetrating floor-sealers with a stain already mixed in. All you do is apply one or two coats of the penetrating sealer to the sanded wood floor, let it dry—and that's it. It's a hard, durable, water-resistant (and washable) finish just as it is. And it's beautiful. (Details on the application are on page 155.) You could, of course, apply a coat of wax to it—or if you prefer a harder, built-up look to the floor, you could apply one of the clear varnish-like finishes over the penetrating sealer. Of course, if you're refinishing a wood floor in the kitchen or an entryway, or wherever water is brought in or splashed about, it's a good idea to put a varnish-like finish on the floor—either over the sealer or on the bare wood. The varnish-like finishes give the *most* water-resistant surface.

Among the clear varnish-like finishes, the hardest-wearing and easiest-to-apply are the polyurethanes. These are sometimes called "polyurethane varnishes"—but these days the term "varnish" doesn't mean what it used to mean; it's become a pretty nebulous term and we don't really have to go into it. Just let it be said that the new products are nowhere near as difficult to apply as the old ones used to be.

Basically, the polyurethanes are made to provide only two

different finishes—high-gloss and satin—though different manufacturers use several different names for them. The high-gloss
finish produces a perennially shiny coating that some people prefer. The satin finish looks more like a mellow, beautifully waxed
surface. Details on the application of clear finishes are on page
157. But the polyurethane finishes made by various manufacturers
are applied differently, so be sure to read the labels carefully
before buying one and especially before using it. Be sure that the
polyurethane finish you buy is one specifically labeled for use
on floors.

There are, of course, other floor finishes. You could use a
lacquer or a shellac or an oil finish. But these finishes are either
more difficult to apply or they don't produce the best-looking and
at the same time most wear-resistant surface. Or, you could paint
the floor with a good, hard, wear-resistant floor enamel. The
directions for doing that are on page 158.

BUT IS IT NECESSARY?

Before you go out and rent a big drum sander and buy your
supplies, take a good long look at your wood floor.

Does it really need refinishing? Or is it just dirty?

Many of us have bought the myth that water must never
touch wood. So we just wax and wax and wax our wood floors
until we're waxing the wax and what we have is a dirty, cruddy
wax build-up that offends the eye. There *is* a way out, short of
refinishing the floor—*wash it*.

But washing the floor needn't mean slathering it in hot, soapy
water and letting the water soak in. Instead, here's what you do:

- Clear the room of furniture. Roll up rugs, move sofas and
  chairs into another room, and otherwise make way for the
  job.

- Mix one cup of a strong detergent such as trisodium

149

phosphate (available as TSP in paint and hardware stores) in a bucket of hot water and apply the solution to the floor with a mop. Also use a good, stiff, old-fashioned scrub brush where necessary.

- Work small sections at a time and dry each section with an old terry towel before starting on a new section. Use another towel when the first one is wet.

- When you've finished washing the entire floor, rinse out the mop, get a fresh bucket of water (cooler, this one) and rinse the floor. Change the water in the bucket from time to time.

- Let the floor dry; remove any black heel marks with fine sandpaper or steel wool.

- Then take another good long look at your floor.

Are there any places where the finish has worn through? If not, maybe all the floor needs is a new coat of wax. But not just any wax. Buy a good paste wax, apply it with a lamb's-wool applicator and then buff it up with a heavy-duty electric floor buffer, which you can rent from a hardware dealer or a tool-rental agency.

Or apply a coat or two of polyurethane finish to the floor. The washing with TSP will have removed the old wax so that the new finish will adhere. Which brings us to Cardinal Rule One for finishing floors.

Cardinal Rule One: Never, *never*, never apply any finish or paint to a floor that has wax or dirt on it. And don't assume that the floor is free of wax if it hasn't been waxed for years. Wax lasts and lasts and lasts longer than any of us thinks it does!

The directions for applying the polyurethane finish are on page 157.

If there are worn spots on the floor, it will probably be a

good idea to sand and refinish it. You could, of course, repair every worn spot by sanding and spot-finishing, and then, when all the spots are dry, apply another coat of finish to the entire floor. But this could turn out to be more work than simply refinishing the whole floor—and you could end up with a mottled-looking result, besides.

However, if the floor was previously finished with a *penetrating sealer,* you *can* then simply sand the worn spots (first with a coarse sandpaper, then with a medium-grit sandpaper, and finally with fine sandpaper), feathering the edges so there's no telltale line of demarcation between where you've sanded and where you haven't. Then wipe away all the sanding dust with a tack rag (which you can buy at a paint or hardware store). Now apply new penetrating sealer to the sanded areas; just apply it with a lint-free cloth, let it dry—and that's it!

SANDING THE FLOOR

Why sand the floor? Because it's the easiest way to get rid of the old finish (including the old wax) and be left with a clean, smooth, level, like-new surface. The sanding process actually removes a thin layer of the wood itself, and in so doing it eliminates imperfections, such as small nicks and gouges, from the surface. Although the work seems to take a good deal of time and bother, it *is* in fact a shortcut. Believe me.

All this is not done by getting down on your hands and knees and sanding away with a piece of sandpaper. As we said, you'll have to rent a big drum sander from your paint or hardware dealer or from a tool-rental agency. While you're renting the sander, be sure you get a demonstration on how to use it as well as a sheet of instructions you can take home with you and refer to as you work.

Also rent an edger and buy a block sander (for the hard-to-reach places) and enough sheets of sandpaper for all the work you have to do. You'll have to take the drum sander over the

151

floor three times: once with coarse open-coat sandpaper, then again with a medium-grit closed-coat abrasive sandpaper, and finally with a fine (100-grit) sandpaper. You'll need the same three grades of sandpaper for the edger and the block sander. Also buy a tack rag to clean up the sanding dust.

Though this costs a bit of money, it's well worth it. And if you decide to redo more than one floor, you can usually rent the equipment over a weekend. You'll need a car or a taxi to ferry it home.

How to sand.   The large sander you have rented has a sort of circular drum on the bottom that spins when the sander is turned on. The sandpaper is attached to the circular drum.

Be sure not to turn the sander on until you're completely ready to begin. That is, clear the room of furniture and take away all the pictures on the walls. Also open all the windows and close all the doors to the room. Stuff newspapers or rags under the bottoms of doors. A lot of sanding dust is going to fly. Cover your hair and wear glasses or goggles to protect your eyes.

Once you're ready to begin—with the coarsest grade of sandpaper on the drum sander—move the machine over to a corner. Do this before you turn on the switch.

At this point, take a last walk around the room and check the floor to see if any nails are protruding. If they are, drive them in with a nailset so they are below the surface. Otherwise, they'll rip your sandpaper to shreds. Then begin sanding, following these steps:

1. Sling the cable over your shoulder so it doesn't get in your way. Turn the sander on and begin moving it *in the direction of the floorboards*, sanding with the grain of the wood.

2. Keep the machine moving once it's turned on. If you leave it in one spot for long, it can damage the floor and leave it wavy and uneven.

3. But then, don't move the machine too quickly along the

floor, either. This makes for uneven sanding. It's best to go slowly, at an even pace, across the entire floor, one strip at a time, as if you were mowing a lawn. If this is your first experience with a sander, move only in one direction—forward—instead of moving back and forth. Sanding is strenuous work and it's complicated enough to control the machine as it moves in one direction without adding the reverse action to your maneuvers.

4. After this first sanding, vacuum up the sanding dust. Now put coarse sandpaper on the edging machine and use it to sand all around the edges of the room on the places the drum sander wasn't able to get to. Start near a corner against the baseboard, working outward to blend in with the wood that has already been sanded. To do this right, you'll have to be in a semi-crouch position with your feet about two feet apart, on either side of the edger. Roll the edger parallel to the wall in small sections. Rest frequently so your back doesn't ache unduly afterward.

5. Again vacuum away the sanding dust. Then place the medium-grit sandpaper on the drum sander and also in the edger and go over the entire floor once again.

6. Vacuum the floor once again. Then empty the bag on the drum sander into a large plastic trash bag or a covered garbage can. Change the sandpaper on the drum sander and also on the edger to the finest grade and repeat the whole process.

7. Vacuum away the sanding dust once again and then take your sanding block and go over any spots you haven't been able to get to with either the large drum sander or the edger. Sand under the radiator as well as in the corners of the room and in the closets. Work first with the coarse, then medium and then fine sandpapers, blending all these small areas with the already-sanded wood. Finally, block-sand with fine sandpaper over the places where the edger was used, for a completely smooth finish.

8. Vacuum again and empty all bags of sanding dust. Vacuum the moldings and windowsills. With the tack rag, wipe the entire floor so it's completely free of sanding dust.

9. Once the room is completely dust-free, you're ready for the next step.

If you don't see the sense of all this work, take heed of Cardinal Rule Two for finishing floors.

Cardinal Rule Two: The better the sanding, the better the finished job.

NOTE: Plan on spending an entire day sanding. If you're really good, maybe it will take only five or six hours.

Important: If you're sanding parquet floors, it's especially important to move the large drum sander in only one direction (forward) and to use *only fine sandpaper. Too much sanding and too coarse a grade of sandpaper can wear down the parquet, which is thinner than other wood flooring.*

New floors. If you're sanding new floors, don't use the coarse sandpaper. Rather, begin with a medium grade of sandpaper in the drum sander and follow by sanding with fine sandpaper.

THE NEXT STEP

If you want your floor just about the color of the bare wood, you can apply either a clear penetrating sealer or you can apply a clear varnish-like finish such as polyurethane directly to the bare wood. The clear sealers and finishes leave the floor only slightly darker than the bare wood . . . about as much darker as if you'd only wet them with water.

If you want your floor moderately dark, you can apply a penetrating sealer that has a stain added to it. You can then either leave the sealer alone or, if you prefer a hard, built-up look to the floor, you can coat it with a polyurethane finish.

If you want the wood to be much darker than it is, you can stain it with a pigmented wiping stain. Over this, you can apply a clear penetrating sealer or a polyurethane finish.

APPLYING THE SEALER

We recommend using a penetrating floor sealer even if you want your floor stained only a little darker than it is. Of all the floor finishes available, the penetrating sealer is the easiest to apply and produces the most durable finish; it is the easiest to clean, the easiest to patch up without leaving any telltale lap marks, and, we think, produces the most beautiful floor finish. As one flooring expert says, applying the sealer requires "no skill, no equipment, and no experience." The secret of penetrating sealer is that it actually becomes part of the wood.

The can of penetrating sealer you buy should indicate that the product can be used for wood floors. It should also say "penetrates," "seals," and if it has a stain, it should also tell you the color of the stain. Some manufacturers make only clear sealers, but a stain can be added to them. If you feel uneasy about adding the stain to the sealer, ask your paint dealer to do it for you. When you get home, try it out on an inconspicuous section of your floor so you can get an idea of what it will look like. If you don't like the way it looks, try another stain. After what you went through sanding that floor, you can afford to waste the price of a can of sealer to get your new finish the right color! As we've already said, if you want your floors stained very dark, you'd best use a pigmented wiping stain.

To apply the sealer, swab it onto the bare wood floor with a brush or a lint-free cloth folded into a pad. Work in strips about two to three feet wide and let each strip soak for about twenty minutes to half an hour (or as the label indicates), and as it soaks into the wood, you can add a little more sealer to keep it wet. *Then wipe it all off.* Then do another strip the same way, and continue until the floor is done. When the sealer is dry enough (the label will tell you when, though it's best to wait overnight), apply another coat again the same way.

Many paint manufacturers put out penetrating sealers and

each product is applied a bit differently. If the label on the can of penetrating sealer you buy gives you directions that differ from ours, follow the directions on the label.

How not to work yourself into a corner: To avoid working yourself into the proverbial corner, plan the job before you begin. Usually, it's best to begin on the side of the room opposite the door through which you plan to exit, and work your way toward the door.

NOTE: Somewhere in your investigations into finishing wood floors, you may have come across a reference to "fillers." In the past, the open pores of wood such as oak were filled and leveled with wood fillers to make them glossy smooth. Hardly anyone is still using fillers these days, however. It is considered preferable instead to retain the "integrity" of the wood. Fillers are definitely not recommended if you're using a penetrating sealer on your floor.

PIGMENTED WIPING STAINS

For dark stained floors, use a pigmented wiping stain directly on the bare, sanded wood. Make sure the label on the can indicates the product is to be used on floors and that it says "wiping" stain. To apply it, use a brush or swab it on the floor with a lint-free cloth, then wipe it off according to the directions on the label. If you want a darker application still, do a second coat after the first one is completely dry. Follow with a clear penetrating sealer or a clear finish such as polyurethane. *Don't* use a lacquer or shellac.

CLEAR, VARNISH-LIKE FINISHES

Today when you go into a paint store and ask for varnish, you'll probably be handed a can that says "polyurethane" or "polyurethane varnish" or, simply, "clear finish." It's enough to say that old-time varnish has been vastly improved upon and that it's not what it used to be—which was difficult to apply. If, however, you're handed a can of "spar varnish," hand it back. It would be fine for your boat if you had one, but not for an interior wood floor.

The new, clear varnish-like finishes can go on directly over bare, sanded wood or over a stain or a penetrating sealer. As we've said, the penetrating sealers don't actually need clear finish over them, but if the *look* of a harder, more built-up finish on the floor is what you want, use one or even two coats. Be sure to wipe the floor well with a tack rag before you apply the finish.

The clear finishes are made in both high-gloss (or high-luster) and satin (or low-luster) varieties. Some manufacturers make an even wider variety of clear finishes, ranging from high-gloss down to flat. The high-gloss finishes produce a perennially shiny coating, while the lower-luster ones yield a mellower surface that resembles a waxed finish. Some require thinning with mineral spirits or turpentine for the first coat, others don't. Be sure to read the label for the thinning recommendations made for the specific product you've chosen.

To apply, brush the clear finish on evenly with the grain of the wood, in strips 2 to 3 feet wide. Use a clean brush of good quality. If you used a lamb's-wool applicator, you would run the risk of applying too thick a coat, which can cause drying problems. If you used a roller, you'd get a stippled, orange-peel effect.

As before, plan the work so you don't paint yourself into a corner. Allow each coat to dry thoroughly (the label should tell you how long the product takes to dry) before applying the next. You may want two or possibly even three coats of finish on the floor. Remember that you must sand each coat lightly with a hand sander and fine sandpaper before applying the next coat.

Important: In general, most clear finishes and polyurethane varnishes should not be shaken in their containers before use. Some may be stirred, but not all *should* be stirred. Be sure to read the label before shaking or stirring. If you've shaken or stirred when you shouldn't have you'll have to wait two weeks for the finish to settle in the can.

NOTE: Pour the finish and any thinner that's required into a pan before you begin and then work from the pan instead of from the can.

WAXING THE FLOOR

Waxing over a floor that has been finished with a penetrating sealer or a clear finish is purely optional. A strictly clear finish does tend to scratch and/or wear away with heavy use, however, so a wax coating will help to preserve it. As one flooring expert told us, "If you wax the floor, the wax will wear away instead of the finish."

The wax may also help to preserve the floor that is finished with only a penetrating sealer if the floor gets exceptionally heavy use. But for ordinary use, waxing is optional. For ordinary maintenance, just dust; or wash the floor if you want to, drying it with old terry towels as you work.

If you wax, be sure to use a good paste wax and put it on with a lamb's-wool applicator. Then buff with a heavy-duty electric buffer. Frequent, once-over-lightly waxing with the "quickie" waxing products on supermarket shelves just causes buildup you don't want.

PAINTING THE FLOOR

Clear finishes are fine, but there are times when a nice, shiny painted floor is better and more fun, such as in a vacation house or a recreation room.

Since painting the floor is a job you surely don't want to do very often, it's best not to take any shortcuts. After you've cleared the room of furniture, wash the floor with TSP and water to make sure you remove any wax that may be on it. And

just because the floor hasn't been waxed in years doesn't necessarily mean the wax is gone. Don't take any chances; paint won't
adhere on a waxed surface. Use one cup of TSP per gallon of
hot water and apply the solution to the floor with a string mop
or a sponge mop and a good stiff scrub brush where necessary.
Work small sections at a time and dry each section with old
terry towels as you work so the water doesn't soak into the
wood. Then rinse the floor with clear, clean water, again drying
as you go. Use dry towels when needed.

The washing with TSP should remove all the wax from the
floor. It should also degloss whatever surface is on the floor.
But if you really want to make sure the gloss is off the surface,
let the floor dry completely overnight and then sand it lightly
all over with fine sandpaper. Vacuum away the sanding dust
and wipe the floor with a tack rag. Then, when you're sure the
surface is as dust-free as possible, apply an enamel undercoater
(one that is meant for floors) with a brush or a roller. If you
use a roller, use an extended handle and be sure the roller cover
has a short nap. Pour out about a pint of the undercoater and
roll it thinly and evenly on the floor in sections, working one
section into another as you go.

Let the undercoater dry completely and then sand it lightly,
vacuum, and dust the surface again with a tack rag. Now you're
ready to apply a good floor-and-deck enamel. Apply the paint
thinly and evenly with brush or roller, thinning with mineral
spirits or water if necessary. You'll want to apply more than one
coat if you don't want to go through this very soon again. We
know one man who put twelve coats of enamel on his floor! It
was beautiful—but twelve coats aren't really necessary to achieve
a beautiful floor. Let each coat dry completely and then sand it
lightly before applying the next one.

TO AVOID DISASTER

These are things to remember, always, when you're finishing
or refinishing a floor.

1. Never paint over a dirty, greasy, or waxy surface. We've said it before but we have to say it again. Just because a floor hasn't been waxed for years and years doesn't mean it's free of wax. It probably isn't! Remove the wax, either with TSP and water or by sanding with a power sander.

2. Never paint over a damp surface—unless you're painting a concrete floor. All wood floors must be thoroughly dry (as well as clean) before any stain or finish is applied to them.

3. Never work when it's raining outside or when there's a great deal of humidity in the air. A friend of ours redid all the floors in his beach house over a long rainy weekend. And then, satisfied with a job well done, he locked up the house good and tight and went back to his apartment in the city. When he returned to the beach the next week, the floors were still wet. In fact, they remained tacky all through the fall and winter until he refinished them the next summer!

4. Don't stint on the job. Don't apply one thick coat of finish instead of two thinner coats. The two thin coats are more durable and dry more quickly than the one heavy coat—which may just remain tacky forever unless you redo the job.

5. Never apply a coat of anything until the previous coat is completely dry. Don't take for granted that a coat of paint or polyurethane or, for that matter, a coat of anything, is dry just because a certain number of hours have gone by. Test the previous coat by pressing firmly on it with your thumb. If your thumbprint shows, the floor shouldn't be recoated. Try pressing with your thumb again in a few hours or the next day. The information on the labels of finishing materials can tell you a lot, but atmospheric conditions make a difference, so be cautious and test.

X

How to Finish &
Refinish Furniture

Fine furniture finishing is an art. So, if your intention is to restore to all its former glory the pricey antique Chippendale table and chairs left to you by your great-aunt Marie, better sign up for courses at the nearest museum offering them, or apprentice yourself to a master craftsman.

However, if your concern is primarily with bargain furniture —the raw-wood kind that you buy unfinished, the worn relics languishing in your cellar or attic, the almost-antique thrift-shop find—you've come to the right place. With a little time, energy, and know-how, you can turn the odd bargain piece into something useful, attractive and—who knows?—perhaps quite special indeed. It needn't be difficult. It can be fun.

FIRST STEPS: GETTING READY

Don't begin any furniture project before you've read through and understood the recommended procedure. Be sure to have on hand all the tools and materials you'll need for the job.

Be aware that many of the products you will have to use are toxic when inhaled to excess and should not be used in a room with all the doors and windows closed. At the same time, dust and other airborne particles that happen to settle on the work in progress—before whatever coating material you're using has had a chance to dry—can mar the good looks of the finished piece. So set up in a well-ventilated but not windy space. And vacuum the area before you start.

The job will at least *seem* easier if you don't have to do a lot of bending and stooping or crawling around on the floor trying to get at the lower sections and underside of a piece. Whenever possible, then, try to bring whatever piece of furniture you're working on up to a convenient height by placing it on a table or workbench, suitably protected with drop cloth or newspapers, of course. To do the underside and legs of a chair, place it seat-side down on another chair (or workbench or table). To do the underside and legs of a table, place it topside down on another table.

To ready the furniture, disassemble it as much as possible. Unscrew knobs, handles, hinges, etc., and keep them all together, along with the screws, in a tin can or a paper bag until it's time to put them back again. Remove doors and drawers and lift out any removable shelves. Tables with leaves should be opened; take out the leaves and set them on the floor or prop them against a wall until you're ready to work on them.

Use newspaper held in place with masking tape to protect the edges of upholstery, mirrors, and other surfaces from contact with paint, paint remover, shellac, or other materials you may be using on the job.

Wear old clothes, of course (including old shoes), and keep a pair of goggles nearby for when you are working with caustic liquids or gels (such as paint remover, etc.) which can drip or splash during application. For obvious reasons, goggles are especially important when you are working with these products at shoulder level or above.

HOW TO SMOOTH AND SAND

Sanding is a crucial step in every single one of the finishing procedures that follow. So, a few words about how to do it properly are in order. True, there are books with whole chapters devoted to specialized sanding techniques, but they are written mainly for those who want to learn the art of fine furniture finishing from A to Z. For the occasional fixer-upper or bargain furniture, the tips below should suffice.

Hand sanding is slower going but preferable to using a disk sander, which contraption has a tendency to go skittering out of control, leaving circular scars in the wood that will only have to be removed afterward by hand anyway. A belt sander is something else again. If you have one and know how to use it, then do so.

Though we speak of "sanding" a piece of furniture, what is properly called—and sold as—"sand"paper is not the best material for the job. Instead, look for and buy garnet or aluminum oxide abrasive papers.

Coarser paper will smooth away irregularities on the surface of a piece, but will itself add fine scratches. The scratches left behind by a coarse paper are in turn removed by a finer-grit paper. That's why it's always a good idea to go over a piece initially with a medium-to-coarse paper (such as 3/0), then switch to finer paper (such as 6/0) for a final smoothing.

It should rarely be necessary to bear down hard on the paper when you sand. Use as little pressure as possible and let the paper do the work for you.

Always sand in the direction of the grain of the wood, wherever it is evident. Cross-grain sanding only roughs up the surface. Sanding with a circular motion is just as bad.

To sand rounded surfaces such as chair or table legs, cut the paper into strips the long way. To use a strip, hold an end in each hand and pull the strip back and forth across the curve.

From time to time on the pages that follow, it will be suggested that you sand lightly between successive applications of a coating. Sanding between coatings helps to insure a good bond between coats and a smoother final finish. "Sand lightly" means just that—a not-too-vigorous going-over with fine-grit paper.

After sanding, vacuum away all particles of sanding dust. This final step is almost as important as the sanding itself. Particles left behind after sanding will interfere with the smooth, even application of the next coating, be it paint, stain, shellac, or whatever. Several of the furniture finishers we talked with recommend going over the piece with a "tack rag" after each sanding. A tack rag is a kind of super dustcloth treated with chemicals that make it pick up and hang on to any loose particles it comes into contact with. Tack rags are available at many hardware stores and paint stores.

HOW TO MAKE A FEW SIMPLE FURNITURE REPAIRS

There's not much point to investing time and energy in finishing or refinishing a piece of furniture that is nonfunctional or otherwise seriously flawed. Take care of repair work first, and do it yourself if you can. Wobbly chair legs; a shaky table top; drawers that stick; loose, bubbled, or missing veneer; dents in the surface—all these are common problems, relatively easy to fix.

Old furniture, of course, is often beset by more serious problems. Most *can* be remedied, but only with an arsenal of specialized tools, materials, and know-how. Such repairs are beyond the province of this book, but there's no lack of good information on the subject for those who are interested. For starters, check out the nearest public library.

1. *Wobbly chair legs.* When chair legs wobble, it's usually because the old glue has given out, or because the wooden legs

have shrunk slightly with age, while the holes into which they are supposed to fit remain the same size.

Either way, if you can possibly do so, completely disassemble the leg from the seat section. Then use an old table knife or similar tool to scrape away all traces of the ancient glue from leg and opening. If you can't disassemble—or don't want to because it seems like too much work—then you must find some way to scrape old glue out of the opening and off the chair leg while the leg remains in place. You might be able to accomplish this by working around in the opening with a nail file.

When the old glue has been removed, you have to reglue. But chances are that the opening is too wide now to afford a good tight fit for the leg—in which case, simply regluing won't solve the problem. You'll have to build up the end of the leg. One way to do this is to wrap some string around it. Next, smear glue into the opening and onto the string-wrapped leg. Plain white glue such as Elmer's Glue will do just fine. Try not to get any glue on other parts of the chair. Insert the leg firmly into the opening and, assuming the fit is snug, that's about it.

But, yes, you should find some way to keep the leg secure in the opening while the glue dries. One way would be to turn the chair right side up and place something heavy on the seat. Lacking several volumes of the Encyclopaedia Britannica for this purpose, you could settle down in the chair yourself, with that novel you've been wanting to read, and stay put for the required time.

2. *Shaky tabletop.*   There are several reasons why a tabletop might be unsteady. Very often, though, the shakiness of a tabletop that is fastened to its base with screws has to do with the loosening up of those same screws. Turn the table over, get a screwdriver, and tighten the screws if need be.

If loose screws aren't the source of the problem, it could be that the top was fastened to the frame or base with glue, and that this old glue is coming unstuck. In that case, clean off old glue and apply new glue. You will probably have to use some sort of clamp to hold the sections together while the glue dries. Often, a C-clamp (available at any hardware store, and handy for dozens of different uses, as you will discover once you own one) will do the trick.

3. *Drawers that stick* often can be made to glide smoothly open and closed if you sand their runners and the tracks along which they move. Sand only enough to get the drawer sliding easily back and forth. Vacuum away sanding dust. Then take an ordinary candle and rub it lightly on runners and tracks.

4. *Loose veneer.* Usually, when we speak of veneer, we're talking about the very topmost layer of wood on a piece. The veneer on a chest or tabletop might be—and probably is—a different kind of wood entirely from what's underneath.

Occasionally, a section of veneer will crack and lift up slightly from the wood under it. When that happens, get a clothes iron, plug it in, set it for medium heat, put a towel or other cloth (folded) over the problem section of veneer, and apply the iron. Heat from the iron may soften and "reactivate" the old glue under the veneer. Take a look under the towel. If the veneer seems to be stuck down again, quickly get something heavy to put on top and leave it there for several hours, until the glue has had a chance to dry. That may be the end of the problem—but only if the old glue is the kind that softens up when heat is applied.

If heat doesn't work, you can try scraping around under the lifted veneer with a nail file or another thin, flexible tool. The object is to try to remove all particles of dirt and old glue; new glue won't stick very well if either are present. Now, spread on some new glue, being careful not to get any on other parts of the piece. Weight the glued veneer with a heavy object for several hours.

5. *Bubbled veneer.* Like veneer that is lifting up from the edge of a piece, a raised, bubble-like section of veneer may re-

quire only the hot iron treatment, plus weight, to press it back down where it belongs.

If that doesn't work, take a sharp single-edge razor blade and slit through the bubble in the direction of the grain. Very carefully scrape around under the veneer to remove old glue. Brittle, dry veneer that threatens to crack with such treatment can be made more flexible by moistening it with water.

When the opening is clean, smear glue under the veneer and weight it with a heavy object until the glue is dry.

The piece will now have a scar, of course. With sanding and painting or repainting, the scar will be far less noticeable. It may even disappear entirely under paint. If you're going to stain the piece and/or give it a clear finish, traces of the scar will remain. Think of it as giving the piece "character" and forget it.

6. *Missing veneer.* When a section of veneer not only loosens and lifts up but breaks off, you will probably be able to mend the damage using one of the two methods described for repairing loose veneer.

But what if you've bought or inherited an old piece from which a section of veneer is missing entirely? In that case, you could do one of two things.

First and best, if you can manage it, would be to patch with veneer stolen from an inconspicuous part of the same piece. If a small section of veneer is missing from, say, a tabletop, you might, for example, be able to cut out and use as a patch a section of veneer from just under the top of the table.

The place in need of a patch is probably of an indefinite, irregular shape. Your first step is to give it a neat, straight-edged shape. (Square, rectangle, triangle—it doesn't matter as long as the edges are straight.) To do this, use a ruler as a guide and score the surrounding veneer with a razor blade. Pry away the scored veneer with a kitchen knife. Clean away all old glue from the newly exposed wood.

Now, with a pencil, transfer to tracing paper the new shape of the section to be patched. Cut out the shape; this is your pattern. Use it as a guide for cutting out the veneer to be used as a patch. But before razoring out the patch, give some thought to grain lines. Ideally, when the patch is glued into place, the grain will run in the same direction as the grain of the rest of the surface.

Try out the patch on the section it is meant to cover. Is the fit good? If not, use a razor blade to make adjustments. Scrape all the old glue from the back of the patch and apply new glue to it and to the section to be patched. Apply the patch, then weight it down with a heavy object for as long as it takes the glue to dry.

If for some reason you can't—or don't want to—patch with veneer from the same piece, you might be able to get veneer from a lumberyard. In order to have a good match, you should of course ask for the kind of veneer on the piece, though this matters only under a clear final finish. Under paint, no one will ever know.

A pattern, as indicated above, will help you get a good fit for the patch. Glue the patch, then weight it with a heavy object until the glue has had a chance to dry.

7. *Dents* in wood surfaces are often surprisingly easy to even out. Here again, it's the clothes iron to the rescue. Plug in the iron, set it for medium heat, place a damp (not dripping wet) folded cloth over the dent and then iron back and forth on top of it. This treatment works because the steam produced by the hot iron and damp cloth goes down into the wood fibers, causing them to swell enough to raise the dent.

PAINT FOR FURNITURE: WHAT KIND AND HOW TO APPLY IT

Most furniture takes a beating. The extent of wear and tear on it depends on what the piece is used for—and, of course, on the people who will use it. A play table in a children's room, for example, is going to get roughed up a lot faster than shelves in the master bedroom. Even so, it's a good idea to use an alkyd enamel on furniture. Though the paint manufacturers are working overtime to improve their latex enamels, the durability, scrubbability and smooth final finish of these products still do not quite measure up to that of the alkyds. Keep this in mind.

If you don't want a very high shine on furniture surfaces, then of course choose semigloss or satin finish enamel; their lower luster is often preferred to the glare of a high-gloss enamel. Also, high-gloss enamels tend to highlight any surface imperfections.

As for using a flat paint on furniture, it *has* been done. But nobody who knows anything about paint *or* furniture finishing recommends it. Flat paint simply doesn't hold up as well under the hard knocks that so many furniture surfaces are subjected to. And besides, although we hesitate to advance the notion that what's usual is always "right" just because people are accustomed to it, the fact is that we're so used to seeing furniture with a bit of sheen to its surface that a flat finish can look strange.

Assuming you're going to go along with the experts and use an enamel on furniture, how do you apply it?

First, see later sections of this chapter concerning patching, sealing, and priming. Then be sure to have a good-quality brush or roller suitable for use with the kind of enamel you've chosen (alkyd or latex) and of a convenient size for working on the piece. Actually, you'll probably need two applicators: a wider brush or roller for large flat surfaces and a narrower one for painting along edges and reaching into hard-to-get-at areas.

One of the possible pitfalls in working with enamel is to lay it on too thinly. Don't overload the applicator, but do flow the enamel on without spreading it out too much. Always use light pressure. If you are using a brush, your strokes should be so light that the bristles hardly bend. Work in smallish sections. Start with light, even, *slow* strokes across the grain. Finish each section with long, even, *slow* strokes in the direction of the grain, gradually lifting the applicator at the end of each stroke.

Every so often, check back to see if the finished work is

smooth and the fresh enamel free of globby-looking runs or "sags." If you see any developing, go back immediately and redistribute the enamel by stroking it lightly and evenly *away* from the problem. It's very important to do this right away, before the enamel has a chance to dry and the sag becomes a permanent feature of the surface.

When possible, position the piece to be painted so that the important large surfaces are in a horizontal position.

In general, the sequence for painting furniture (or for applying any coating material) is to turn the piece over and do the underside and/or legs first. That way, you not only get the hardest part over with, you also have a chance to practice and to get the feel of the wood and the way it takes to the material you are working with. By the time you are ready to do the more visible top surfaces, you'll know how and when and if to adjust your work to get a smooth, even finish.

Do interior surfaces—the insides of bookshelves, cabinets, cupboards, etc.—before exteriors. Otherwise, there's a greater risk of smudging a freshly painted outside (and yourself) in attempting to reach in and do the inside of a piece.

How many coats of enamel? Two, probably. It's doubtful that you'll get good, even coverage with one coat only unless you're painting white enamel over a white undercoater.

When two coats are necessary, allow the first coat to dry thoroughly. Then sand lightly (vacuum or use a tack rag to remove all particles left by the sanding), before applying the second coat.

HOW TO PAINT UNFINISHED FURNITURE

When we refer to unfinished furniture, we mean those pieces made of "virgin" wood to which no paint, shellac, wax, or anything else has ever been applied.

1. *Check the surface* to make sure that it is smooth and clean. If the piece is brand new, it's probably free of heavy accumulations of dirt, but it will surely need a good sanding. Sanding, since it removes some of the surface, will also remove much surface dirt along with it, so in a sense this is a two-in-one operation.

Start with 3/0 paper, then switch to 6/0 paper for a final smoothing. As you sand, slightly round off any edges that are very sharp. A sharp edge may have a nice, neat appearance, but the finish won't hang on to it as well as to a somewhat softened edge.

2. *Vacuum* and/or use a tack rag to get rid of sanding dust.

3. *Check the piece for knots.* If you see any, give the piece a coat of pigmented shellac sealer (also called "stain-killer). This material not only will prime the wood for painting, but also will seal the knots. Knots left unsealed may leak sap which will ultimately work its way up through the finish paint and create unsightly stains.

As of now, pigmented shellac sealer comes in white only. If you are planning to use a dark-colored finish paint, it will be worth the extra trouble to tint the sealer to more closely approximate the finish paint. (The finish paint will cover better over tinted sealer.) Sealer can be tinted with universal color (see page 39) in the appropriate shade. Add universal color only in the proportions suggested on the tube or can it comes in.

4. *There may also be fine cracks* where there are knots in the wood. After applying the shellac sealer, use spackling compound to fill in any cracks or holes. (Follow instructions on the label.) Allow ample time for the spackle to dry. Sand the filled areas, then prime again with a coat of pigmented shellac sealer.

NOTE: Wood that is entirely free of knots can be primed with an enamel undercoater instead of pigmented shellac sealer. Like the sealer, enamel undercoater comes in white only but can be tinted with universal color. If necessary, thin the undercoater according to instructions on the label.

5. *Sand again.* When all areas of the primed piece are thoroughly dry, give it a light sanding. Then vacuum or use a tack rag to get rid of sanding dust.

6. *Apply one or two coats of enamel.* When the first coat is thoroughly dry, sand lightly, then apply the second coat.

HOW TO REPAINT FURNITURE

Here, we're talking about putting a fresh coat of paint on furniture that has been painted previously—or finished with shellac, varnish, etc.

1. *If the piece is very dusty*, vacuum it. Then wash it with a detergent solution, rinse it with a cloth wrung out of clear water, and wipe it dry.

2. *Use benzine or paint thinner* to remove every last trace of wax or polish from the piece. Wipe the solvent on with a cloth, rub vigorously, then wipe clean with another cloth. Both solvents are highly flammable; observe all safety precautions listed on the label.

3. *Check the piece for surface damage.* Fill any holes or cracks with spackle. Holes or cracks that go down to the bare wood should be spot-primed with a coat of shellac before you patch with spackle.

4. *If the old paint is chipped*, use abrasive paper to smooth away the sharp edges and blend in the chipped area. If the

chipped area remains very noticeable, fill it in with spackle. A chip that exposes bare wood should be dabbed with shellac before spackling. It is not necessary or desirable to "take the paint down" to the bare wood. Smoothly sanded, the old paint will add "body" to the new.

5. *Certain stains can't be painted* over successfully; they work their way up and discolor the finish paint. Since it's hard to tell beforehand which stains have this annoying ability to bleed through, it's best to block all stains with a coat of shellac. Let this dry thoroughly.

6. *Sand the entire piece*, paying special attention to spackled areas and other surface irregularities.

NOTE: Don't skip this preliminary sanding—not even if the old surface is unmarred and perfectly smooth, and no patching was necessary. Paint failure—flaking, peeling, etc.—is often the result of applying new paint directly over a glossy old surface that lacks the "tooth" to hold on to it. Sanding roughens up the surface enough for the new paint to stick.

7. *If the old surface is intact* and needed no patching with spackle, you can go ahead and apply a first coat of enamel now.

However, you'll get better coverage and a longer-lasting, smoother-looking new finish if you first lay on an application of an enamel undercoater. (As we said earlier, the undercoater can be tinted with universal color.) If you decide to use the undercoater, allow it to dry, sand lightly, then proceed with one or two coats of enamel.

8. *If the old surface was patched* with spackling compound, the patches should be spot-primed. You can spot-prime by dabbing a thin coat of shellac on each patch. When the shellac is dry, sand it. Then, either finish up with one or two coats of enamel or apply an enamel undercoater first. The undercoater really will give you better results in the long run. When the

undercoater is dry, sand lightly, then apply one or two coats of enamel.

Or, instead of spot-priming patches, you could use pigmented shellac sealer to prime the whole piece. In that case, there would be no need to use an enamel undercoater. The sealer, remember, can be tinted with universal color. When the sealer is dry, sand lightly, then apply one or two coats of enamel.

HOW TO PAINT WICKER

For the past few years, wicker furniture has been all the rage. Made of woven strips of cane, rattan, bamboo, reed, etc., wicker presents a very different kind of surface from that of most other furniture, and a lot of people approach the painting of wicker with trepidation, if at all.

Wicker *does* present some special problems. But it can be painted, and with great success. The important thing about painting wicker is, of course, to make sure that all the intricately woven strips are evenly covered. Working with a brush requires patience and a constant eye out for skips. You may prefer to spray-paint a wicker surface because the mist will carry through easily to places that are hard to reach with a brush.

1. *Go over the piece lightly* with fine- to medium-grit abrasive paper. In the case of wicker, you are sanding not so much to smooth the surface as to slightly roughen it up so that you'll get good paint adherence no matter what the old finish (if any) may be. Don't rub too hard; let the paper do the work for you. And make sure you've covered every inch of the piece.

2. *Vacuum* away every last trace of sanding dust.

3. *Apply a coat of pigmented shellac sealer.* As you no doubt know by heart by now, it comes in white only, but can be tinted to approximate the color of the finish paint.

If you own a spray gun, you might want to use it to apply the sealer. (See spray-painting techniques, page 64.) Use denatured alcohol to clean the gun when you are finished.

If you work with a brush, you may find that a gentle scrubbing motion, or light jabbing at the surface with the bristles of the brush, helps to work the sealer into intricately woven spaces. But don't make the mistake of glopping on too much sealer (or, later on, finish paint). A too-heavy application may run and/or bridge the spaces between the woven strips, making parts of the surface look all of a piece. And when this happens, the characteristic light and airy look of wicker is lost.

4. *Allow ample time for the sealer to dry.* Sand lightly. Then vacuum away sanding dust.

5. *Apply one or two coats of enamel.* Two light coats are always better than one heavy coat, and this is especially true on wicker. Sand lightly and vacuum away sanding dust between coats.

HOW TO STAIN UNFINISHED FURNITURE

Once again, we're talking about nude wood that has never been treated to a coat of paint, stain, varnish, shellac, wax, or anything else.

But before you go ahead and stain unfinished furniture, ask yourself whether it had better be painted instead. Knots in the wood are not necessarily a problem. Stain won't completely conceal the knots, of course, but a knotty pattern can be quite interesting. However, much unfinished furniture is made of poorly matched wood or of "wild-grained" wood that will not take a uniform stain. The final result of attempting to stain such wood may be an unattractively mottled or murky surface.

How can you tell whether a stain will "take" nicely on the

piece in question? If sections of the unfinished piece are very much lighter or darker than others, it's doubtful that you will be able to stain it in such a way that the color is completely evened out. But even unfinished wood that *looks* uniform in color can be a problem. If you're in the process of buying a piece, ask the salesperson whether it is of "stainable" quality. If the piece is one you've had for a while, just be aware that the final results of staining it could be quite beautiful, on the one hand—or rather disappointing, on the other.

There are many different kinds of stain made to darken or tone or otherwise add color to bare wood surfaces. There are stains with a water base and stains that are dissolved in alcohol or oil; there are stains that add color only, and stains that penetrate and seal the wood as they color it. Some you have to mix up yourself. Others require only that you open the container and apply the material properly.

There are advantages and disadvantages to using each type, but when applied according to the manufacturers' instructions, any of them will give good results on good wood. However, professional finishers tell us that the kind of stain that falls into the category of "pigmented wiping stain" is the easiest and most foolproof for the novice to use.

A pigmented wiping stain probably will not have that designation on the label. In fact, if you go into a paint store and ask for one, as we did, the salesperson may look at you as though you'd taken leave of your senses. Not many people call it that. How, then, are you to know a pigmented wiping stain when you see one? First of all, ask for a small can of interior wood stain and read the label. If the instructions include the directive to stir well before applying, and if it says farther down to wipe the stained surface with a cloth after a certain number of minutes have elapsed, you have a pigmented wiping stain. The method of application of these stains varies somewhat from brand to brand, so follow the instructions given on the label.

One more suggestion before you begin: The final color of the stained wood surface will depend to a great degree on the natural color and density of the wood itself. In other words, the shade you selected as most appealing when you saw it on a color card at the paint store may not be the shade you end up with. To get a better idea of what the final color will be, try out the stain on an inconspicuous part of the piece. If you're not satisfied with that color, you can lighten or darken the stain, add more red or yellow—or tone out some of the red or yellow—by mixing in some other stain of the appropriate color(s). Just stick with the same brand. Of course, you could also go out and buy another can of stain in a different color and try *it* out.

In any case, it is always difficult if not impossible to exactly match a piece of unfinished furniture to some already-finished piece that you have. Aim for color harmony instead.

1. *Sanding.* Since the wood stains we're concerned with here are at best only semi-opaque, and the wood itself will remain on partial view underneath, it's very important to start off with a clean surface. If you're working with a brand new piece of unfinished furniture, chances are that a good sanding will be all that's needed to get rid of smudges and surface dirt. Remember to sand with the grain, not against it. Start with a medium-grit paper and finish with one that has a fine grit.

Unless you're going to use the sanding dust for patching (see below) vacuum it all away.

2. *Patching.* Now is the time to take care of cracks and other openings in the surface. A new unfinished piece should have few of these, though there may be problem areas around the knots (if any).

Before you decide to fill in every hairline crack on the piece, be forewarned: No patching material yet invented will take stain in exactly the same way as the wood. (How could it? No two woods take stain in exactly the same way, either.) This means that unless you are willing and able to touch up patched areas with the same painstaking exactness as the counterfeiter employs in his art, the patching material will stand out as being more or less unlike the rest of the surface.

With the foregoing in mind, here's how to fill in the cracks, gouges, and other openings that are worth bothering about.

If the piece you are working on is made of pine (as of now most furniture sold unfinished is made of this wood) you can patch with a cellulose-fiber filler, such as Plastic Wood. Plastic Wood has particles of pine as a major ingredient and therefore takes a stain at about the same rate as pine. That means there should be a minimal color difference between the patch and the rest of the furniture surface after the stain has been applied. Use the filler according to instructions on the label. Sand it when it is dry.

If you are working with another kind of wood, you might want to patch with sanding dust (saved from sanding that same piece) mixed to a paste with animal ("rabbit") glue. The paste should be more sanding dust than glue. Press it down firmly into openings in the wood. Allow a day or so for it to dry. Then, with a razor blade, carefully slice away any excess. Use fine-grit abrasive paper for a final smoothing.

(NOTE: A third patching alternative would be to fill in with wax sticks *after the final finish has been applied*. Wax sticks are available at many hardware stores and paint stores. They come in a variety of colors. If none of those colors comes close to the color of the stained piece, you can melt together pieces of two or more different-colored sticks for an almost-perfect match. To patch with wax sticks, you must first melt them in the bowl of a spoon or some other small vessel. Then carefully drizzle the melted wax into the crack or gouge to be mended. Use a knife blade to shape and press the still-liquid wax into the depression. Finally, scrape away any excess.)

3. *Staining comes next.* If mixing is called for (as it most certainly will be if you are using a pigmented wiping stain), give the stain a thorough stirring. Use a good brush or a soft, clean

cloth to apply the stain with the grain of the wood. Start in an inconspicuous spot, so that you'll get the feel of working with the material and can judge the rate at which the wood drinks up the stain. Then move on to major visible areas of the piece.

Aim for a thorough, even application. You don't want to have one area soaked to excess, with others barely covered. Work carefully and quickly. You'll get the best results if no one area is allowed to dry too much before adjacent areas are covered. For this reason, always do one whole surface or section at a time. Finish one entire side of a chest, for example, before moving on to another side.

Whenever possible, turn the piece so that you are working on a horizontal rather than a vertical surface. When you must work on the vertical, apply the stain from the bottom up.

Follow to the letter the manufacturer's instructions about how and when to wipe off excess stain. They vary. Keep in mind that most stains will dry lighter than they appear to be when wet, and that in general, the longer excess stain is allowed to remain on the piece, and the less you wipe off, the more intense will be the color. Apply a second coat in accordance with the directions on the label.

4. *When the second coat is dry*, you can use cheesecloth or some other soft, clean cloth to buff the piece to a satiny, natural wood glow.

Although there's no law that says you *must* apply a clear finish over stained wood, you probably should do so to shield the surface from dirt, grease, and damage caused by various liquids, etc.

CLEAR FINISHES AND HOW TO APPLY THEM

Clear finishes protect wood surfaces and add sheen—or in some cases a really glossy shine. You can put a clear finish over a stain, or—with the exception of wax—over a clean, properly prepared bare wood surface. (Some people say wax is no exception to the above, either.)

Actually, the clear finishes that go on bare wood aren't perfectly clear, after all; it is not true that they in no way modify the appearance of the wood. Most of them will darken or slightly intensify the color to about the same degree as would a damp cloth wiped across the surface.

There's a wide variety of clear finishes from which to choose. Before you make a final decision, if you are working on a piece you have just stained, take another look at the label on the stain container to see which, if any, clear finishes the manufacturer specifically recommends for use with the product. Just as important, take note of any warnings *against* the use of certain finishes.

It seems that almost every professional furniture finisher has his or her own pet recipes for concocting various kinds of clear coatings. But the finishes we are going to be concerned with here are the kind that you can walk in and buy right off the shelves of any reasonably well-stocked hardware or paint store.

1. *Paste wax.* A coat of paste wax will give a subtle sheen to the piece and offer *some* protection from water and other liquids. Apply it with a soft cloth and a *lot* of elbow grease. Or, attach a wax applicator to a ¼-inch drill and let the machine do most of the work for you.

One expert tells us that many people try to get the wood to accept too much wax at once, which makes the job harder than it needs to be. "You shouldn't spread the wax like butter on bread," he says. "Instead, take a golf-ball-size lump, fold a damp cloth around it, and squeeze the wax through the cloth. What comes out is enough to start with."

2. *Oil finishes.* There's a kind of mystique about the hand-rubbed oil finish. Nothing, it is said, quite equals its durability and the soft natural glow it brings to the wood surface. But achieving it is hard work.

You can use warmed boiled linseed oil. (It comes boiled; don't boil it yourself. As for warming it, do *not* set it on the stove. Put it in a container, then set the container in a pan of hot water.) You can use a mixture of approximately two parts boiled linseed oil to one part turpentine, also warmed (but not on the stove). You can use tung oil. You cannot use salad oil, or mineral oil, or most oil-base furniture polishes. None of the latter harden as they dry, which is what linseed oil and tung oil will do and which is why they are used for this purpose.

What do you do with the oil? You put a liberal amount of it directly on the clean, very smooth wood surface. Then, using a soft, lint-free cloth, you rub it in hard. And keep on rubbing and rubbing. Some say to rub the same section for at least fifteen minutes, then wipe off any excess. Others say to rub until the wood will absorb no more oil, which probably amounts to about the same thing. Either way, you have to rub one section for a long, long time before moving on to the next. The oil is allowed to dry for a day or so, and as it dries it hardens. Then a second coat is applied. Then a third if you want to go through the process all over again.

Or, if you want the protection and natural good looks of an oil finish, but not all the hard work, search the shelves of your local hardware store or paint store. You will probably find, not too far from the boiled linseed oil, the tung oil, and the turpentine, a section stocked with the new "instant" oil finishes. If you decide on one of these, apply it according to the instructions on the label.

3. *Shellac.* This gives a lovely, rich, glossy finish to a stained piece. It "excites" the grain pattern and the color of unstained wood.

The good news about shellac is that it's easy to apply. The bad news is that a shellac finish is easily marred by alcohol, soap or detergent and water, and sometimes just plain water, which makes shellac a less than ideal finish for utilitarian pieces such as coffee tables and dining-room tables and chairs. However, a shellac finish might be just the thing for a cabinet or bookcase that would not normally be exposed to spilled liquids.

Look for white (clear) shellac that says "3-pound cut" on the label. The "cut" refers, among other things, to the consistency of the shellac.

One other important thing to consider when buying shellac is its freshness. Shellac that is more than, say, six months old probably won't dry properly. For this reason, always look for a date on the can of shellac you are about to purchase. Or, buy from a store that does a large volume of business in wood finishing products and which would thus (presumably) have only fresh shellac on its shelves. If in doubt about the freshness of shellac, brush some out on a piece of scrap wood; if it doesn't dry hard and smooth within an hour or so, don't use it on the piece you're finishing.

Assuming you've bought 3-pound-cut shellac, the first coat should be thinned with denatured alcohol. A good first-coat consistency would be three parts shellac to four parts denatured alcohol.

Wipe the surface to be coated with a tack rag before you begin. Then, with a brush, flow the shellac on smoothly in much the same way as you would enamel. Work quickly, but don't slap it on. Slapping it on may cause surface bubbles. If you see bubbles forming, smooth them out by going over them lightly with just the tip ends of the bristles.

You should apply at least two coats. Three would be better. Allow the first coat to dry (complete drying time is in the neighborhood of two hours), then go over the piece lightly with fine-grit abrasive paper. Clean the surface with a tack rag. Then apply a second coat of shellac, this one straight, not mixed with denatured alcohol. Sand again before applying a third coat.

Denatured alcohol is used for cleanup after shellac.

If you like, you can apply a coat of paste wax to a shellac finish. Just wait until at least twenty-four hours after the final coat has dried.

4. *Lacquer* is the finish used on most mass-produced furniture today. With lacquer, you get a strong, quite glossy surface that is less vulnerable to spills, etc., than shellac. You could, in fact, put a coat of lacquer over a shellac finish to toughen it up.

The trouble with lacquer, though, is that it dries so quickly that the novice may have difficulty brushing it out to a smooth, even finish. There are lacquers called "brushing lacquers" that have been modified to make them dry more slowly—but not *that* much more slowly. Their application is still a problem.

The ideal way to apply lacquer is to spray it on; at least that's how the big furniture manufacturers do it. But they have elaborate facilities to spray safely (lacquer is highly flammable) and well. You'd have to improvise.

The experts we spoke with have said, in effect, Why bother with lacquer when there are other, easier-to-apply finishes around?

5. *Varnish* means different things to different people. Indeed, if you go into a hardware store or a paint store and ask for "some varnish" it's anyone's guess what you will get. The salesperson might, for example, hand you a can of polyurethane varnish, which can be used on stained or bare wood interior surfaces. Or, you might be given a can of spar varnish, which certainly should not be applied to any indoor surface, but would be just the thing for your boat, if you have one.

There are so many different formulae for modern varnishes that it's not easy to characterize the material, except to say that a varnish finish on furniture has good heat and water resistance, doesn't scratch easily, and isn't much affected by alcohol and most other spills. Of all the different kinds of varnishes, polyurethane (a can of which may not even have the word "varnish" on its label) is toughest.

If you want a durable surface, and you like a slightly "built-up" look (as opposed to the "natural" bare- or almost-bare-wood look of a wax or oil finish), varnish might be your best bet. Just be sure to buy the kind that is made for use on *interior* wood surfaces. Many varnishes are available in glossy and semigloss formulations. Some polyurethanes come in finishes that are almost flat.

Old-time varnishes are said to have been notoriously difficult to apply because they dried so slowly. Under certain circumstances, drying time could drag on for so long that dust and other particles in the air would build up on the still-tacky finish and ruin it. Modern varnish products are much better in this respect. However, it's still best to apply them in an environment that is as nearly dust-free as possible. Vacuum the room before you apply the varnish, then wait a while for all the dust to settle before you get to work. Just before you begin, wipe the piece with a tack rag.

If you're going to be varnishing a large piece, start off by pouring some of the varnish into a small container. Then put the lid back on the large container so that it is not exposed to air for long periods.

Some manufacturers recommend thinning the first coat of varnish with an appropriate solvent. (If you are using polyurethane, the solvent will most likely be mineral spirits.) Check the label to see whether such thinning is suggested for the material you have chosen.

Varnish should be flowed on smoothly, not slapped back and forth like paint. The theory is, the less brushing you do, the better the final finish. Start each stroke in a dry area, and brush back into the previous wet one.

If you can manage it, work with the surface between you and a source of light. That way you'll be able to detect any bubbles, skips, or runs as they occur. These can be remedied immediately by going back over them with an almost-dry brush, using long, light strokes with the tips of the bristles and gradually lifting the brush at the end of each stroke. (If you don't get back to these problems right away, don't do anything at all about them. You can smooth them out with abrasive paper before you apply the second coat.) Check the label to see how long to wait before sanding and applying a second coat.

HOW TO STRIP PAINT AND OTHER OLD FINISHES

Getting the old finish off is by far the most odious step in fixing up furniture. Nobody—but nobody—actually seems to like doing it. True, some of the new paint-stripping products have made the job easier and less hazardous than ever before. But stripping is still unpleasant work. So before you begin to remove an old finish, ask yourself whether it really needs to be done.

If you're simply going to put a new coat of paint on a painted piece, you don't need to strip off the old finish first. Just sand that old paint well, patch it if necessary, then prime and paint according to the step-by-step instructions for painting finished furniture (page 169).

When *is* stripping necessary? When you want to put a natural (stained or clear) wood finish on a piece that has been painted, or when you want a natural wood finish and the old wood finish on the piece is in such bad shape it just won't do.

You could sand away or scrape away an old finish, or even remove it by means of heat (special tools are needed for the latter). Some old-timers swear by lye. With just the right light touch you might be able to do a fairly good job with one of the new mechanical paint-stripping devices that are attached to a ¼-inch drill. With this last, however, there's always the possibility that the wires of the device (which literally "lash" the paint off the surface) will chew too deeply into the wood, leaving hard-to-remove scars.

In the long run, a chemical paint-and-varnish remover is probably the best choice. Most will lift and dissolve paint, varnish, and shellac and lacquer as well. Some will also remove stains from an old wood surface.

For safety's sake, buy the kind of remover that is nonflammable. Another advantage to most nonflammable removers is that they are of a thick enough consistency to hang on to vertical surfaces without running off down the sides. When you buy, search the label to see whether the remover requires special cleanup (or "neutralization") with paint thinner or some other solvent before a stain or clear finish can be applied to the piece. Some brands need no such cleanup; in choosing one of them, you save yourself a step.

Methods for using paint-and-varnish removers vary somewhat depending on the type and in some cases the brand you have selected. Always use these products exactly in accordance with the instructions on the label, and heed all safety precautions suggested by the manufacturer. These include, among other things, working in a well-ventilated area (the fumes can be quite harmful) and rinsing away with water any of the chemical that may come in contact with your skin. Not included on all labels, and well worth mentioning here, is the need to wear goggles to protect your eyes from splashes and fumes. Goggles are especially important if you are applying remover to surfaces higher than shoulder level.

Protect the floor with drop cloths and/or layers of newspaper. Have several empty coffee cans on hand into which you can sling the sludge when it has done its job. Set chair and table legs in coffee cans; that way, you can simply scrape finish and remover down each leg and into the can.

Apply a generous coating of remover with a brush. Here's one instance where a cheap brush is fine. Stroke the remover on in one direction only. Avoid painting back and forth or otherwise disturbing the remover once it's on the surface; moving it around exposes more of the remover to air and this slows and interferes with the chemical action. (To minimize exposure to air, some pros suggest covering the fresh application of remover with aluminum foil or waxed paper.)

You will know the remover is doing its work when the old finish looks wrinkled or bubbly. This will take from ten to thirty minutes—possibly longer—for most removers. When you see the bubbles or wrinkles, take a putty knife and, working *with* the grain of the wood, push the sludge from one end of the surface to the other end, and off. No scrubbing or rubbing—just pushing —and be careful not to dig into the wood with the putty knife. You can use an old toothbrush, or fine soapless steel wool, or a bit of steel wool wrapped around a pencil or a toothpick to work sludge out of corners and carved areas.

If, after you have pushed the sludge off, the surface is almost entirely free of finish, use steel wool to help the remover along with the few stubborn spots that remain. But if the remover stripped away only one of what appear to be several layers of paint, and there is still a long way to go before all the bare wood is exposed, don't bother with steel wool now. Lay on another thick coat of remover. Depending on how many layers of what kind of finish is on the piece, it may take two or even three applications to do the job.

When all the old finish has been stripped away, wipe the surface with fine steel wool, then a clean cloth. Follow the manufacturer's instructions for any additional steps that may be required to condition the surface before proceeding to refinish the piece.

XI

Special Effects

Usually, people do a paint job because the surface or piece in question—ceiling, wall, floor, table, chair, whatever—is beginning to look somewhat the worse for wear. Or, because a coat of fresh, new color would add new life to a room or object. But there's another type of painting project that has to do with creating effects that are out of the ordinary—special effects, if you will. Some of the most charmingly subtle or eye-catching and dramatic decorative touches in your home can be achieved with paint.

You don't need an artist's talent for the special effects that follow. Simple antiquing, stenciling, spatter painting, and other techniques collected in this section are all relatively easy to achieve, assuming you're willing to put forth the effort to work carefully and correctly.

Antiquing (a commercial, somewhat inaccurate word) apes the softened colors, the subtly grained texture, the gracefully faded, shaded, and aged look of fine old furniture. The technique probably won't fool anyone into thinking that your five-dollar thrift-shop chair is really an heirloom—but then it isn't supposed to. Antiquing is simply a way of adding surface interest to what might otherwise be a ho-hum piece of furniture. Furniture isn't the only thing you can antique. You can do the same thing to wood paneling, doors, built-in cabinets and cupboards, and other wood surfaces as well.

You can antique a freshly painted piece, or a piece with an old painted surface. Or, you might want to fool around and see what happens when you antique a stained wood surface.

Probably the simplest way to do antiquing is to go out and buy a kit. These kits are quite popular; almost every major paint company packages one. A kit will save you the trouble of having to assemble the required materials yourself. Also, there's practically no way to go wrong with a kit—assuming, of course, that you follow carefully the instructions that come with it.

Antiquing kits vary in their contents. Depending on the manufacturer, a kit may contain every single material and tool you'll need to complete the job. Or, you may have to supply brushes, cloths, and one or two other things yourself. When you buy a kit, read the instructions to find out what, if any, additional items you will need to purchase.

However, you don't need to buy a kit to do antiquing. You can buy the materials à la carte and probably save yourself some money in doing so.

What should you get? Some alkyd enamel to start off with. The enamel corresponds to what is called the "base coat" in many kits. The color of the enamel will be the basic color of the finished piece. If you have just finished painting a piece in alkyd enamel, you needn't repaint; just apply glaze (the essential step in antiquing, about which more later) over the new enamel surface. You could also use glaze over an old painted surface, or over a stained surface; the only requirement is that the painted or stained surface be clean and free of materials such as wax and oil.

Next, you need a glaze. You can go into most well-stocked hardware or paint stores and pick up a can of glaze right off the shelf. Glaze is a tinted transparent coating that is brushed on, then, after a few minutes, brushed or wiped off again to produce any number of shaded or grained effects.

Buying glaze is a lot easier than mixing it up yourself. But it's worth noting that you *can* make your own. And if you do, you can get "custom-color" effects that might not be possible if you rely on the ready-made glazes.

To make your own glaze, mix 1 part linseed oil with 3 parts mineral spirits, then stir in one or more different shades of universal tinting color. How much color should you add? As much as you need to get the effect you want. A good idea is to paint some scrap lumber with the same alkyd enamel that you used on the piece you want to antique. Then try out small quantities of various glaze mixtures until you hit on one that you like.

A few words about color here: Theoretically, you can put glaze of any color over any shade of enamel or stain. But some of the most pleasing results are achieved by using glaze colors that are reminiscent of natural wood shades—even over surfaces that have been enameled green, red, blue, or some other decidedly unwoodlike color. Wood shades can be obtained by mixing in various amounts of two or three of the following universal tinting colors: raw umber and burnt umber (brownish); burnt sienna (reddish); yellow ocher and chrome yellow; orange; black; white.

If you are antiquing or "shading" a surface that has been finished with a wood stain, you'll probably want to use a glaze that is a somewhat darker version of the stain color. In fact, assuming you've used an oil-base pigmented wiping stain on the surface, you can use that same stain to make a glaze. Just thin the stain with mineral spirits, add universal color to darken it, and stir in some clear varnish. (Make sure the varnish is the kind that can be thinned with mineral spirits.)

Whatever the glaze color, be aware that it will look lighter when it dries than when it has first been applied and wiped off the surface.

If you're going to use an antiquing kit, then of course follow the instructions that come with it. If you've decided to assemble your own "kit," follow the step-by-step antiquing guidelines that follow:

Prepare the wood surface, then apply enamel—or stain— according to the methods outlined in Chapter X.

When the surface is completely dry, brush on the glaze, one section or surface at a time. Don't try to cover too much territory at a time. Don't apply the glaze to *all* the paneling in a room at once, or to an entire table or chest. Do work in sections: one panel or a part of a panel; a tabletop; the side of a chest.

While the glaze is still wet, take a soft cloth and wipe some of it off the surface. Where you wipe, you get highlights—areas that have just the slightest hint of misty-looking glaze color that are a pleasing contrast to the shaded, unwiped areas.

The usual method of antiquing, producing the most-often-seen effect, is to wipe much or practically all of the glaze from the center sections of large, flat surfaces (the top of a table, for example, or the top, front, and sides of a chest, etc.). Gradually lift the cloth as you approach the edges and corners; these are left unwiped or only very lightly wiped, as are surface details such as carvings, moldings, etc. The idea is to blend the highlighted areas with the darker, shaded ones in such a way that there are no harsh lines of demarcation.

Don't wipe off too much glaze at first, not even from the areas you want highlighted. Now take a look at the result. (Remember, the glaze will dry lighter than it looks when you first apply it.) If you decide you want less glaze (more highlight) on certain areas, quickly wipe more of it off. If you want more glaze (deeper shading), allow the surface to dry, then brush on another application. If, after the surface is dry, you decide that you'd like less glaze, you can remove some of it by rubbing gently with fine steel wool.

But that's just the beginning. If you want a subtle wood-grain effect instead of simple highlighting and shading, you can go over the wiped but still-wet glaze with a *dry* brush. Use the tips of the bristles only. One knowledgeable amateur tells us that her favorite graining effects are achieved by first brushing lightly across the surface *with* the grain of the wood, then, after waiting a few minutes for the wet glaze to "set up" or get tacky, brushing against the grain.

Other interesting effects can be had by wiping the glaze with a circular motion instead of in long back-and-forth strokes. Some people like to do the initial wiping with a dry brush instead of a cloth; this gives a slightly streaky appearance that can be quite attractive. Still others have experimented with other wiping materials—fine steel wool, for example, balls of crumpled newspaper, or just about any flexible material that can be drawn across the glazed surface without damaging the wood.

If the final effect is not to your liking, remember that you can go back—*when it is dry*—and remove some or most of the glaze by rubbing with fine steel wool. Then reapply it in a different way. When you're satisfied with your handiwork, you can give the surface some kind of clear protective finish, though you really don't have to. Wait until it is thoroughly dry.

Striping is still another way to make something special and, yes, unique, of an unremarkable painted surface.

The kind of striping we're talking about here is simple edge lining with paint. This is usually done about an inch or so from the edges of a piece of furniture or other painted surface. Just about anyone who is reasonably steady of hand can manage it and do it well. (Far more elaborate striping effects can be achieved, but they require a good deal of practice to perfect.)

1. Prepare the surface of the piece. If an old painted surface needs repainting, turn to the appropriate chapter to see how it's done. Even painted surfaces in good condition should be washed with a detergent/water solution. Rinse, then wipe dry. If the surface has been waxed, rub vigorously with mineral spirits and a cloth; go over the surface lightly with soapless steel wool; then wipe with a clean cloth. (Heed all safety precautions on the label when working with mineral spirits.)

2. Now give the surface a coat of shellac. This is one of the really important tricks of the trade. If you make a mistake on a shellacked surface, it's very easy to wipe the paint off and start over again.

3. Buy or make a striping brush. Many stores that carry a full line of furniture finishing products will have striping brushes in stock. These are most often made of squirrel hair and have a distinctive, long, tapered-to-a-point shape. If you can't find such a brush, don't worry. A friend who does fine furniture finishing for fun and profit makes her own striping brushes.

First, she pulls a few bristles from an old natural bristle brush. With cotton thread, she ties these bristles to the end of a kitchen match. Then she applies white glue—sparingly—to further anchor the bristles to the match. When the glue is dry, the brush is ready to use.

NOTE: The more bristles you use in making a striping brush, the wider the stripe it will apply. You can also investigate water-color brushes in an art-supply store.

4. Use alkyd enamel thinned with a small amount of mineral spirits. Experiment to get a good consistency. The enamel you use for striping should be thin enough to flow freely off the brush, but not so thin that it dribbles.

Load the brush by dipping it almost up to the top of the bristles. Wipe off excess enamel against the edge of the container. Have a sheet of paper handy; make one or two practice stripes on it after each loading of the brush. These practice stripes are important because they remove more enamel from the brush. Too much enamel and it may come gushing out from the bristles, causing a big, fat bulge in the stripe.

5. With index finger and thumb, hold the brush in an almost horizontal position. Your other three fingers should overlap slightly the edge of the surface to be striped. Always draw the brush toward you. As you do, those last three fingers act as the guide, moving along the edge of the surface you are striping and keeping the brush parallel to that edge—even if it is a curved edge.

6. When the striping is done and the enamel is completely dry, you might want to apply a protective finish to your work. Once again, polyurethane varnish is a good choice. Use it according to instructions on the label.

Spatter finishes may be the most fun of all and often yield the most spectacular results—but with spattering, you never know for sure what those results will be until you're finished!

Subtle, slight spattering gives an attractive "distressed" (aged and gracefully timeworn) look to a piece of furniture. This technique is often used in antiquing—after applying the base coat, but before brushing on the glaze. To do this kind of spattering, you will need an old toothbrush and some black paint. Thin the paint just the slightest bit; use water to thin latex paint, mineral spirits to thin alkyd paint. Dip the toothbrush into the paint. Then flick your finger, or a twig, or a Popsicle stick in an upward direction over the bristles. The result should be a fine spray of tiny black droplets on the piece.

Do experiment first, however. The thickness of the paint, the flexibility of the brush (or its lack of flexibility), its distance from the target, as well as your aim and manner of directing the spray will all affect the results. Practice on brown paper bags or cardboard until you can control the spatters and reproduce certain spray patterns at will.

You can make bigger spatters with a bigger brush. Some people work with a small scrub brush. Others like to use a trim brush or wall brush, or artists' brushes of various sizes. When working with brushes larger than a toothbrush you'll need some kind of stout stick. A dowel or a section of a broom handle works well.

Load the brush and grasp the stick in one hand; then, with the other hand, strike the brush smartly against the stick. Paint will fly off the brush on impact and, assuming your aim is true, will spatter onto the surface you want to decorate.

As with any other kind of painting, spattering should be done only on a clean, wax-free surface. Wash an old painted surface with a detergent/water solution, then rinse and wipe dry before spattering. If you suspect wax has been used on the surface, rub with mineral spirits on a cloth, scrub gently with fine soapless steel wool, and wipe dry.

Otherwise, there are no hard and fast rules about spatter finishing. You can spatter almost any kind of surface—including floors and walls—with almost any kind of coating material, from latex and alkyd paints, to enamels, to glazes, and so on. Some of the most interesting effects have been achieved with the most unlikely materials and in the most extraordinary color combinations. (If you plan to spatter with more than one color, allow the first color to dry before applying the next—unless you want the colors to run together. On second thought, why *not* allow colors to run together and see what happens?)

The key to it all is experimentation—that, plus a trial run on a practice surface before trying out materials and color combinations on any possessions you really care about.

When the spatter finish is completely dry you may apply a clear protective coating. Polyurethane is a good choice. Use it according to the instructions on the label.

Stenciling is quite an old decorative form which is now fast regaining popularity, as well it should. It's a relatively easy method of adding color and pattern to a piece of furniture, a wall, even a floor.

In fact, in some parts of the country (or at least in our part of the country—New York City and thereabouts) the stenciled floor is enjoying quite a vogue. More and more small companies and individual craftspeople are specializing in floor stenciling that duplicates the look of a beautiful area rug—the "rug" being done entirely with paint.

Regardless of the surface to be stenciled, the procedure is always basically the same:

1. Choose a background color, prepare the surface to be stenciled, then paint it. (If you are stenciling a piece of furniture, see Chapter X for how to paint it; refer to Chapter IV for how to

paint a wall; and for how to paint a floor, see Chapter IX.)

NOTE: If you want to stencil over an old painted surface, you can do so. Wash it down first with a detergent solution and water, then rinse and wipe dry. Again, if you have any reason to suspect that there may be a residue of wax on the surface, wipe it with benzine or mineral spirits on a cloth (remember, these solvents are flammable; use them with care). Scrub lightly with fine soapless steel wool. Wipe dry.

2. Buy or make stencils.

Many art-supply stores sell ready-made stencils, but you can certainly make your own. Look through magazines or art books for appealing designs in appropriate shapes and sizes. Or, use your imagination and sketch a design. (Unless you're gifted in this area, stick to simplified, easily recognizable forms.)

Transfer the design to tracing paper, then cut it out carefully with scissors. This cutout design is your pattern. Lay it on a piece of stencil paper (available at art-supply stores) or sturdy cardboard large enough to accommodate the design with plenty of space to spare. (Warning: Don't use corrugated cardboard; it's much too heavy to work with.)

Trace the outline of the pattern onto the stencil paper or cardboard, then cut it out. Use a single-edge razor blade, a mat knife, a pair of small sharp scissors—any tool that will enable you to get a neat, clean edge without unduly bending the stencil.

3. Place the stencil on the surface to be decorated, then use masking tape to hold it securely in position.

NOTE: Don't apply masking tape to any surface that was painted less than a week before, or the tape may take some of the paint with it when you remove it.

4. Apply the design.

Use a special stencil brush (many paint stores carry them, as do most art-supply stores) and alkyd enamel paint. Pour some of the paint into an old saucer or other shallow container. Dab the bristles into the paint, then dab on a paper towel to remove any excess. Apply the paint to the surface with an up-and-down dabbing or tapping motion. Don't attempt to flow the paint on. Don't

196

use back-and-forth strokes. Just dab or tap the paint on, or you run the risk of smearing it under the edges of the stencil. If that happens, it's good-bye clean, recognizable design and hello mess.

5. Wait until the paint used for stenciling is completely dry, then remove the taped-on stencil. If the design needs touching up, or if you want to add more detail, now's the time to do it. Use an artist's brush and alkyd enamel in the appropriate colors.

6. When the paint is dry, apply a clear protective coating to your work. Polyurethane varnish is used most often for this purpose. Apply it according to instructions on the label.

NOTE: If you want to decorate a surface with repeated stenciled motifs, cut as many duplicate stencils as you will need to get all the stenciling done in one operation.

For designs that require two or more colors, cut a stencil for each color. Always let the first color dry before applying the second. Multicolored stenciling can get to be a complicated proposition, though. It must be carefully planned; you will probably need to make a small preliminary sketch, to scale, of where each form and color belongs.

Wall graphics are those big, bold, colorful designs that are painted on walls, ceilings, or both, livening a room like nothing else. You've probably seen them—if not in person, then in the pages of your favorite decorating magazine.

If you like the look of wall graphics, you may want to invest in a kit telling how to do them. But a word of warning here: These kits are relatively expensive, considering that all you get are instructions for a few different designs. You have to buy paint and other materials and supplies separately.

You probably can design and then paint your own wall graphics without a kit. If there's enough of the artist in you to *want* a wall graphic, you probably can.

One young father we know decided to do something special with his baby daughter's room. First, he painted the room with pale-blue latex paint. Then, a couple of days later when the paint was completely dry, he took a pencil and went to work, lightly sketching on the walls a waist-high garden of daisies, tulips and tall grass that extended all the way around the room. When he was satisfied with his sketch, he took paint—two shades of green for the leaves and grass, white and yellow for the daisies, red and yellow for the tulips—and colored in his design. No, the flowers, leaves, and grass were not botanically correct, but the effect is all the more charming for that.

Of course, what he did was more a wraparound mural than wall graphics. That term brings to mind geometric shapes and designs—giant arrows, numbers, letters, bull's-eyes, stars, stripes, etc. But the basic idea is the same: applying a painted design to a painted wall or ceiling to add a splash of extra color and dash to a room.

If you want to do a wall graphic of your very own, the first step is to figure out a design. Make a sketch. Make several sketches. Keep in mind that although big, bold swirls and irregular shapes of color, done freehand, may *seem* more difficult to execute, they are actually easier in the long run than geometric shapes because geometric patterns require plumb-straight lines and perfect proportions in order to look well.

Many people like to use graph paper to plan a design. Thus, they can make a scale drawing of the design and its placement on wall or ceiling. Measure the wall or ceiling, or both. Then, for simplicity's sake, let each square of the graph paper represent 1 square foot of wall or ceiling space. (Don't forget to indicate windows, doors, and other surface features on the graph paper.) Now, draw your design to scale.

Since color is integral to any design, make color decisions next. Remember that you can more easily paint a bright- or dark-colored design over a light background, than you can a light-colored design over a dark background. In fact, you may be able to get good one-coat coverage of dark over light. But you'll certainly have to apply at least two coats (possibly three) to get good coverage of light over dark.

NOTE: If you feel you just *must* have a light-colored design on a dark background, apply a first coat of pigmented shellac sealer to the design area. The sealer will help prevent the background color from bleeding through and may save you the trouble of having to apply several additional coats of finish paint.

As for what kind of paint to use—latex or alkyd; flat, glossy, or semigloss—the choice is pretty much up to you. In making the decision, keep in mind that the glossier the paint, the more obvious will be any little imperfections on the surface and in the execution of the design. On the other hand, shiny paint definitely packs a bigger visual punch and can be wiped clean a lot more easily than flat paint.

When you've decided on a design and the color(s) to use, the next step is to apply the background color. Paint walls and/or ceiling according to the step-by-step instructions given in Chapter V.

NOTE: Allow new paint to dry for at least twenty-four hours —longer is better—before applying your design to the surface. Check instructions on the paint label.

But *must* you apply a new coat of paint? What if you simply want to paint your design on a previously painted surface? Then go ahead and do so—but only if the existing paint is in good shape and the surface is intact, with no cracks or holes in evidence. (As always, if you do decide to execute your design on an old painted surface, wash it first with a detergent/water solution. Rinse. Then wipe dry.

Now it's time to transfer your design from graph paper to painted surface. This may be the hardest part of all, but there are a few simple tricks to make it easier.

Horizontal lines are relatively easy to mark if you use kite string as a guideline. First, consult the graph-paper design for the exact location and positioning of horizontal lines. Let's say your design calls for a horizontal line three feet up from the floor and running all the way across one wall. Measure up three feet from the floor at one end of the wall. Mark lightly with pencil. Measure up three feet from the floor at the other end of the wall and mark. Now tape kite string from mark to mark. (The string must be pulled taut.) Dot lightly with pencil at short intervals along the string. *Voilà!* You've marked off a perfectly straight horizontal line.

Vertical lines can also be marked off with the aid of kite string. Check the graph-paper design for proper positioning of vertical lines. Make a light pencil mark at the highest point of each vertical. Then tape a length of *weighted* kite string over each mark. (You can weight the string by tying any small heavy object to one end.) Dot lightly with pencil at short intervals along the lengths of string.

Circles. Again, use kite string; this time it will act as a kind of compass. Determine the size and exact location of each circle by referring to the graph-paper design. Mark a dot on the wall at the exact midpoint of the circle you wish to draw. Now, tie a length of string tightly and securely around a pencil. (Fasten the string with tape if necessary.) Measure and snip the string to exactly half the diameter of your circle-to-be. With one finger, hold the end of the string over the dot. With the pencil in your other hand, pull the string out as far as it will go. Now draw. If you keep the string taut, you'll outline a perfect circle. (Could be that two people can do a large circle better than one.)

Arcs. An arc is just a segment of a circle. Use string for a compass and draw as before.

Free-form designs, as we said, don't require the same careful plotting, measuring, and marking as do straight lines and circles. Use your graph-paper design as a rough guide in transferring shapes to the surface to be painted.

Finally, paint the design. You can apply masking tape along the straight lines of the design. This will help you get a neat, clean painted edge—but only if the tape is pressed down firmly enough to prevent paint from running under it.

NOTE: Don't apply masking tape to any surface that was painted less than a week before. Tape has a tendency to take new paint along with it when it is removed. Pull tape off the surface soon after your painted design is thoroughly dry—certainly within twenty-four hours of applying it. The longer tape stays on a surface, the more difficult it will be to remove.

Paint circles and other curved areas of the design freehand. Do outer edges first. An artist's brush with long, flexible bristles is a good tool to use here. Start each stroke slightly away from the edge. As the brush makes contact with the surface, twist it slightly so that the bristles are folded into a point. Outline with the point, then switch to a trim brush to fill in.

Work slowly and carefully. If you make a mistake, don't despair; just clean up quickly. (Use a cloth and water for latex paint cleanup, a cloth and mineral spirits for alkyd paint.)

XII

Painting All the Rest

There are many, many objects around the house that you may want to paint and that we haven't mentioned yet. So here goes for as many as we could think of:

Andirons and other fireplace accessories of the cast-iron or steel variety. Brush with a wire brush to remove any loose particles, then clean with paint thinner (mineral spirits). Be sure to take precautions when working with paint thinner, as it is highly flammable. Don't work anywhere near an open flame; open the windows for adequate ventilation. If they are previously unpainted, prime the andirons or other fireplace accessories with metal primer and paint with a flat or glossy heat-resistant metal paint. Black is the best color to use, as it won't show the smoke stain. If the accessories have been painted before, you can omit the primer. If the previous paint was glossy, sand with medium-grit sandpaper to degloss the surface before repainting.

Old bathtubs, sinks, and laundry tubs. Porcelain enamel sinks and tubs that are worn thin and stained can be respectably refurbished with an epoxy paint of good quality. First wash out the tub or basin with detergent and hot water, and rinse. Then make a paste of powdered pumice stone (which is available in most hardware stores) and water. Rub this over the entire surface with a cloth to roughen the surface so it will hold paint and to remove any traces of soap film. Be sure to rub the area around the soap dish especially well. Work the pumice into any stains— particularly rust stains and those green copper-pipe stains around the drains and faucets. If the stains are stubborn, add some heavy-duty scouring powder (such as Ajax or Comet) to the pumice paste to give it a little extra power, and scrub with steel wool. If you can't completely remove the stains, don't be overly worried; but give it a good try. Then rinse completely and let the tub or basin dry before painting.

Epoxy paint is quite difficult to apply, particularly because it dries so quickly, but it yields a strong, glossy, water-resistant finish that wears like iron. Be sure to buy the best epoxy paint you can afford. It comes in two cans, and the contents must be mixed together before it can be used; follow the directions on the label with the greatest care. Since you're working indoors (unless you remove the tub and take it outside to paint!), it's best to brush the paint on rather than to spray it on, which creates too much overspray indoors. Since the paint does dry so quickly, don't let *anything* interrupt you as you work. Don't even stop to answer the phone. Clean up any drips or spills immediately with a special epoxy thinner you should buy at the same time that you buy the paint. And don't expect to use the paintbrush again. Once epoxy paint starts hardening, there's no stopping it; it will harden completely. Always work with the windows and doors wide open.

If you're painting an old tub or basin that has a metal outer surface, that can be painted too. Wipe down the metal with paint thinner to remove any grease or dirt, then wipe away the paint thinner with a damp cloth. If the metal is unpainted, coat it with a metal primer. Then paint with a good alkyd enamel. If the metal has been painted before, sand the surface before painting.

Blackboards. Blackboards can be repainted, and new blackboards can be made on just about any smooth surface—wood, metal, cardboard cartons, wallboard, etc.—with special blackboard slating. This paint is difficult to find, however, and not just any black (or green) paint will do. A blackboard has to be erasable as well as washable. After trying four or five places, we finally found a can of Gillespie's Blackboard Slating (made by the Klean-Strip Company of Memphis, Tennessee) in a small, well-stocked paint store where the man behind the counter seemed to know everything there is to know about paint.

Blackboard slating must be stirred thoroughly before use. When you buy it, ask the paint dealer to jiggle it for you on a machine that's usually kept behind the counter; then stir it again yourself before you paint. (Or "box" the paint, according to the directions on page 25 in Chapter I.)

The paint should be applied lightly and evenly to a clean, dry surface with a flat, *fine*-bristle brush (but not so fragile as camel's-hair). For maximum durability, three coats of paint should be applied about forty-eight hours apart, according to the directions on the label. The first coat is applied a bit more thickly than the others. Each coat of blackboard slating must be sanded lightly before the next is applied. If the paint in the can gets too thick because of evaporation, it can be thinned with a little (but not too much) turpentine. Turpentine is also used for the cleanup.

Brass, bronze, and copper.   We don't believe in painting over brass, bronze, or copper. We don't even recommend covering these metals with lacquer because, somehow, a little tarnish always seems to sneak in under cracks in the lacquer—and then, if you want to shine them, the lacquer has to be tediously removed. Let them be.

Closets.   You can paint closet walls as you would paint any wall. But when the closet is small, be sure to take frequent breaks from the work and keep nearby windows—and of course the closet door—wide open so you get adequate ventilation.

To reach the upper recesses of the walls and the ceiling as

well, take out any shelves and move a ladder into the closet. Again, climb down the ladder and out of the closet at frequent intervals for some fresh air. If the closet is too small for a ladder, use an extended roller or an extended paint pad for the uppermost reaches, and "cut in" the corners as best you can. If painting the ceiling is a problem, don't paint it. No one will ever know. (When I lived in New York and my apartment was painted by a professional painter, hired by the owners of the building, there was no way you could get him to paint a closet, let alone a closet ceiling. Maybe he was just being logical!)

If you have been able to remove the closet shelves, wash them with detergent and water, and if they have been painted previously with a glossy paint, degloss it with sandpaper. Prime the wood if it has never been painted before. Then apply a semigloss paint to the shelves, or use the same paint you used on the walls. Semigloss is preferable, as you will probably want to wash the shelves eventually; doing so might even eliminate the need to repaint them sometime in the future. Semigloss on the *walls* could serve the same purpose—permitting a good washing to take the place of repainting later on.

Electric switch plates. To avoid getting paint on a switch or outlet, always remove the switch plate before painting it. If you're painting the wall at the same time, this will prevent painting the plate to the wall, which would make it difficult to remove without damaging the paint if your outlet ever needs repair. Wash the electric switch plates with detergent and water to remove fingerprints and dirt, dry them, sand them, prime them with an appropriate primer, and paint. Either use the same paint you've used on the wall or, if the wall isn't painted, use a high-gloss alkyd paint or enamel so the surface can easily be wiped free of fingerprints. Be sure to paint the heads of the screws that hold the plate to the wall. By the way, the purpose of painting switch plates is to make them look well (unobtrusive) with the color scheme of the room. Buying a new one won't help unless its commercial finish happens to suit you.

Formica and other plastic laminates. If you *know* you can't live with your plastic-laminated surfaces the way they are, paint them. First wash the surface with TSP (trisodium phosphate, available in hardware stores) and water—one cup of TSP per gallon of warm water. Then rinse the surface and wipe it dry with a clean cloth. To give it a little "tooth" so it will hold the paint, sand it lightly all over with fine sandpaper. Then prime it with a pigmented shellac-base sealer, which dries quickly and will bond to the plastic laminate so that you can paint over it with any paint you want. For most purposes, the best paint to use is a high-gloss alkyd enamel that washes easily and takes a good deal of wear and tear. Apply it with a brush. The shellac-base sealer dries to the touch in fifteen minutes and can be painted over in about forty-five minutes. It thins with denatured alcohol, which is also used for the cleanup.

If the plastic laminate is around a sink, however, it's best to use an epoxy enamel for the top coat(s). Epoxy yields the most water-resistant finish. When using it, be sure to follow the directions on the container as carefully as you can. Work quickly, with no interruptions, and clean up immediately with epoxy thinner, which you can buy when you buy the paint. Plan on throwing your brushes away once the job is done, however. They'll be impossible to clean!

Heating registers. If you don't like the color of your heating registers, you can paint them easily. But before you begin, remove the registers by unscrewing the screws or bolts that hold them in place (keeping the hardware in a paper bag until you're ready to replace it). Then dust the registers thoroughly, wash them with detergent and water, and let them dry. Sand the existing finish once-over-lightly with sandpaper, wipe away the sanding dust, and then paint with any paint, latex or alkyd, that you choose. If you spray-paint, take the registers out of doors or down to the basement and work there. Or contrive a spraying booth out of cardboard as described in Chapter III.

If, however, there are rust spots on the registers, remove the rust with sandpaper or steel wool, then prime the registers with metal primer before painting.

Metal shower stalls. If the finish on the metal has chipped or cracked or seems to have worn thin (which often happens if the stall is not of the best quality), clean the shower stall thoroughly by wiping it with a strong detergent or with TSP and water. Rinse thoroughly (by running the shower) and dry with old towels. Then sand away any rust and prime the entire stall with damp-proof red primer. Paint with a high-gloss enamel formulated for use on metals. Over red primer, you may need two coats. (For adequate ventilation as you work, keep the bathroom windows and door open, and take frequent breaks.)

Nursery furniture and toys. A few years back, when the anti-lead laws were enacted, all *interior* paints were made safe for use on children's furniture. Clean the furniture before painting or repainting; sand and prime appropriately. (See Chapter XI on finishing and refinishing furniture.) Apply a durable, washable, high-gloss paint that will take a lot of wear and tear.

Pianos. If the piano is a treasured musical instrument, it's wisest to let a professional refinisher paint or refinish it for you.

But if it isn't particularly valuable, you *can* refurbish the wood yourself. If the veneer is chipped and gouged and you'll have to do a good deal of patching, you'll probably be happiest with the results if you apply an opaque enamel or high-gloss paint rather than a clear finish. Be especially careful to keep the paint out of the sound box and off the keyboard.

Before you paint, clean the surface thoroughly with mineral spirits (paint thinner) and reglue any loose veneer. Fill in missing veneer and gouges (see Chapter X on furniture refinishing), then sand the filled-in areas so they are smooth. Then sand the entire surface lightly and apply an enamel undercoater or primer. When this is dry, sand it with fine sandpaper and apply your top coat. Again, take care to keep the sanding dust out of the sound box; keep your vacuum cleaner handy. Tape newspaper over the keyboard if there is no cover for it. To achieve a hard, durable finish, you may have to apply two or three thin top coats, being sure to sand with fine sandpaper between each coat.

If, however, the wood is in good shape and you decide to apply a clear finish, follow the same steps you would to refurbish old furniture, as described in Chapter X.

Ping-Pong tables. A Ping-Pong table that can still stand up straight is definitely worth repainting. But first, wipe the table down thoroughly with mineral spirits (paint thinner) and sand it lightly all over with fine sandpaper. Wipe away the sanding dust with a tack rag. Cover the white lines completely with masking tape so you don't paint over them—pressing the tape down along the edges so the paint won't seep under. Then brush or roll on a good flat green latex paint. With the help of a color chart, you can closely approximate the color already on the table and, possibly, do the job with only one coat of paint.

Be sure to remove the masking tape as soon as the paint is dry, as the tape is difficult to remove if left on for long. Then either touch up or completely repaint the white lines, if necessary, with flat white latex paint. If you have a reasonably steady hand, you can probably do the job without the help of a straight edge, since the lines are already on the table. Don't apply masking tape to the freshly applied green paint to help you with the white lines. Masking tape has a tendency to take new paint along with it when it is removed.

Stairs. Paint or finish stairs as appropriate to their material (masonry, wood, etc.)—but so you don't strand yourself in case you have to run up or down those stairs before they're completely dry, make it a two-part job. First, paint every second stairstep— and when those steps are completely dry, paint the ones you didn't paint before. Be sure not to paint the railing at the same time you paint the stairs, or you'll have nothing to hold on to while you're double-stepping up and down the stairs. This system is better than first doing one side of each step, then later doing the other side, because it avoids a "seam" where the two coats of finish overlap at the center.

XIII

The Front Door

The scope of this book was purposely limited to interior painting. The line had to be drawn somewhere. Since exterior painting requires different materials (and, to a degree, different tools and procedures), it seems logical to draw that line at the front door. But there are two sides to a front door. Rather than leave it half finished, here's how to paint the other side of the front door, the outside.

First, a little story about a young couple who cared enormously about the appearance of their home. They had chosen a marvelous charcoal-gray latex paint (flat) for their living room and entryway. They put the same charcoal-gray latex paint on the interior side of their front door. So enamored were they with the color and the smooth, problem-free application of the paint that they decided to use the same paint on the exterior surface of the door, as well as on the modest porte-cochère sheltering the front porch.

It didn't work. They painted in early fall. By midwinter, the charcoal gray interior paint on the exposed exterior surfaces began to give out.

The moral: If you put paint intended for interior use on exterior surfaces, you're asking for trouble, even if the exterior surfaces are sheltered from the elements.

Paint products intended for exterior use will have the word "exterior" prominently featured on their labels. Don't use any other kind for painting out of doors.

NOTE: The same rule holds true for materials other than paint, such as varnish. Exceptions will be indicated on labels.

You can, of course, put interior paint on the *inside* of a door leading outside. But what is the best material for painting the outside of your front door? An exterior enamel—no doubt about it—unless you want a clear finish on a wood door. In that case, use a varnish suitable for exterior surfaces. (We'll have more to say about varnish later.)

As for color, it has long been standard to use one color on all exterior trim surfaces. But for the front door, trim color or another color is the question. It's your decision—and besides considering how a door color looks on the facade of the house, you can also think of how it looks when the door is opened into the entryway.

Once you've chosen what paint and color to use on the outside of a door, it's time to go to work. Or is it? What about the weather?

How hot or cold or wet or dry it is outside is only occasionally relevant when you're working on interior surfaces. But it does make a difference when you paint exteriors. Obviously, you're not even going to be tempted to paint outside when it's raining. But rain falling from the sky is only one consideration. Exterior painting is one of the few endeavors to which the old injunction "There's no time like the present" definitely does not apply—certainly not if "the present" happens to be a muggy summer day with lowering skies. Or even a clear, dry day, if the weatherman predicts late afternoon showers. Moisture in the air while the paint dries can interfere with good final results.

Wind is a factor, too. On a windy day, grit and other atmospheric particles may be blown onto fresh wet enamel and become embedded there for the life of the paint job. Avoid painting when

211

insects are at their peak; otherwise they, too, may get caught in the still-wet enamel.

As for temperature, check the label on the container. Some materials should not be applied when the mercury drops below a certain point.

It may sound as though you're never going to get your front door painted. Not so. But you may have to wait until fall, which is the ideal time for exterior house-painting in most of the United States.

Now assuming weather conditions are right, how do you proceed? Very much as you would if you were putting enamel on an interior trim surface. Preparation comes first.

HOW TO GET THE DOOR READY
FOR PAINTING

1. Remove as much hardware from the door as you possibly can. Painting is always faster and easier when there are few or no obstructions such as doorknobs, escutcheons, etc. Certainly, you should take down the house number if it is screwed on or otherwise detachable. If you can't or don't want to remove the other hardware, protect it with plastic wrap secured with rubber bands. Or, resolve to paint *very* carefully around it. It's generally not a good idea to use masking tape on exterior surfaces, especially those that are in direct sunlight; exposure to sun seems to make it all the more difficult to remove any residue left by the tape.

2. Use a whisk broom to get rid of dust.

3. If there's a heavy accumulation of greasy dirt, wipe the door with a cloth saturated in mineral spirits. Then wipe it dry with a clean cloth.

4. Inspect the doorframe. If there are gaps where the frame meets the exterior wall of the house, clean out the crevices (a wire brush comes in handy here, but any tool that can be used to scrape out debris is fine). Then wipe out the area with mineral spirits. Finally, use caulking compound to fill in the gaps. Make sure you

get the right kind of material for the job. Follow label instructions for proper application.

5. Use putty to fill in any small holes or cracks on the surface of the door. Brush away any debris in the opening. If the bare wood is exposed, spot-prime first (use shellac or whatever primer is recommended by the manufacturer of the enamel), *then* putty. When the puttied areas are dry, smooth with sandpaper so that they are even with the rest of the surface.

6. Sink any loose or bulging nails to about ⅛ inch below the surface. Spot-prime the holes, then fill them with putty. When it is dry, smooth it with sandpaper.

7. Scrape away all chipped or peeling old paint. Use sandpaper to blend in the edges of these areas. You don't want hard lines showing through the new enamel.

8. Wash the entire surface with a detergent/water solution. Rinse, then wipe dry.

NOTE: If what looks like dirt on the old surface doesn't wash off with detergent and water, that "dirt" might be mildew. Scrub with a mixture of 1 quart chlorine bleach, ⅓ cup detergent (make sure you do *not* use a detergent containing ammonia; mixing ammonia and bleach is dangerous and always to be avoided), and ⅔ cup trisodium phosphate stirred into enough warm water to make up a gallon of solution. This solution will do away with mildew already on the door, but to prevent new mildew from growing, use a paint containing a mildewcide. (Also available are mildewcidal agents that can be added to some paints. Ask your paint dealer about these.)

9. Go over the entire surfacely lightly with sandpaper. This final step ensures a good bond between the old finish and the primer.

But is a primer really necessary?

Yes, if you're painting light over dark. Yes, if you're painting a previously unpainted surface. Yes, if you're painting over varnish. And yes, if you want best results. Check the label on the can of paint or enamel you plan to use to see what kind of primer the manufacturer recommends.

Now, here's the procedure for painting the door:

If the door has a window, start there. Paint the muntins (the narrow strips separating the panes) if any; then paint the molding around the glass.

Panels, if any, are next. Start with the molding around each panel, then move to the panel itself. If paint begins to collect at the corners of a panel, quick, before it starts to dry, go back and redistribute the paint away from the corners with long, light strokes.

Now paint the raised surfaces. Finish with long, light, cross-wise strokes on the horizontal crossboards; use long, light, up-and-down strokes on the verticals. You can get a smoother, stroke-free finish if you gradually lift the applicator at the end of each long, light stroke.

A flush door can be painted in the same manner as any large, flat surface. Work from top to bottom. Finish with long, light strokes. Gradually lift the applicator at the end of each stroke.

NOTE: You can get good coverage of the hinge if you paint it first with the door closed. Then open the door to paint the rest.

Do the edges of the door. First the top edge, then the two long vertical edges. But if the exterior of the door is to be painted one color, and the interior another, you will be painting only one vertical edge now—the edge closest to the hinge, if your door opens *into* the house.

Finish with the frame. Work horizontally across the top, then down each side.

HOW TO VARNISH AN EXTERIOR DOOR

If your door is wood with a clear varnish finish, here's how to prepare it for revarnishing:

1. Wash it down with a detergent/water solution. Rinse it and wipe it dry.

2. Go over the entire surface with sandpaper. Sanding will rough up the old varnish finish enough to provide a good bond

for the new varnish. Brush away every last trace of the sanding dust.

3. Apply the varnish. Make sure it is the kind that is suitable for exterior surfaces. Check the label for application techniques specific to the brand and type of product you are using. Work quickly. Follow the sequence suggested before for painting a door.

What about patching nicks, gouges, cracks, and scratches in the old finish? Many minor surface imperfections will be less noticeable when the new finish is dry; they may not need patching.

But an old finish that is in *very* bad shape should be removed. Use a chemical paint-and-varnish remover. Read carefully and follow to the letter all instructions on the label. Then apply new varnish.

However, if the surface of the door itself is in such poor shape that major patching is necessary, you're probably better off forgetting about varnish entirely. Any attempt at patching, unless it is done with the greatest care and skill, will almost certainly call attention to itself and be clearly visible under a clear varnish finish. Better to patch, and then go ahead and *paint* the door.

Index

217